IT'S ONLY A BIKE RACE:
HOW HARD CAN IT BE?

Touring France with the world's premier cycling endurance event

Steve Banner

Banner Business Services

Fort Worth, TX

Steve Banner/Banner Business Services
Fort Worth, TX
www.itsonlyabikerace.com

Front cover design by Holly Sosa.

Book Layout © 2014 BookDesignTemplates.com

It's Only A Bike Race: How Hard Can It Be?/ Steve Banner. -- 1st ed.
ISBN 978-0-9864341-0-5

For David Vale, who opened my eyes to the world
beyond my island home.

"It is by riding a bicycle that you learn the contours of a country best, since you have to sweat up the hills and coast down them."

ERNEST HEMINGWAY

CONTENTS

OVERVIEW OF 2014 *TOUR DE FRANCE* ROUTE

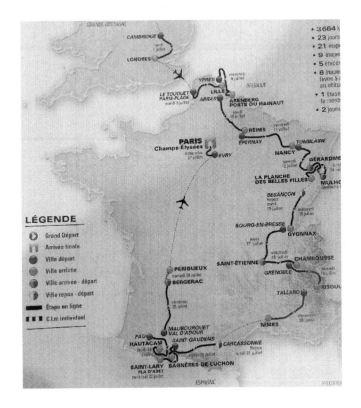

YOUTHFUL DREAMS OF FRANCE

"Ride a bike around France for a few weeks? What a great idea! We'd get to see France and maybe even get our names in the paper." Secure in the vast store of worldly knowledge that we had acquired by the ripe old age of 13, my friend Tony and I fancied ourselves as being capable of almost anything we set our minds to. Our bikes were our constant companions as we explored our neighborhood on the western side of the city of Adelaide in South Australia, and they were our main form of transportation to our basketball games, the beach and of course school. With broadly similar geography to Los Angeles, Adelaide is located on a flat plain with the sea to the west and hills to the east. However unlike Los Angeles, Adelaide in 1969 had a population of fewer than one million people. Traffic on the roads was therefore not heavy and the flat landscape made it a perfect environment for Tony and I to ride our "deadly treadlies" (as we called them) to every place our youthful whims led us.

In May of that year I had begun studying French at high school. The class was taught by David Vale, an energetic and very capable English immigrant in his late twenties who also taught German and Latin. My two older sisters had studied French before me at the same school under other teachers, but Mr. Vale's 1969 first-year class was different because we would be the first class ever at Findon High School to use the new French curriculum known as "*Ecouter et Parler*". This curriculum, whose title translated to "Listen and Speak" in English, was revolutionary for its time because it was based around a series of reel-to-reel tape recordings that the teacher would play to the class. Mr. Vale was clearly excited about using this new system, and his enthusiasm carried through to his students. Being a natural mimic since my early childhood, this teaching approach was a natural fit for me as it was based around us repeating the sounds, words and phrases that we heard on tape. French quickly became my favorite subject and before long I became curious to learn more about the country of France.

Sure enough after several months the curriculum started to incorporate segments about France and the lifestyle of the French people. Photographs in the text book were used to stimulate discussion, and among the black-and-white pictures of delicious-looking pastries, pretty countryside and ornate buildings, there were a couple of pictures of gentlemen riding old-fashioned-looking bikes. Mr. Vale explained to us that these men were participating in the "*Tour de France*", which he further explained as an event that lasted several weeks and involved riding a bike around France. At first I thought he meant that it was a marathon event in which the participants rode from sunrise to sunset without a break, but when he told us that the bikes were only ridden for a few hours each day I realized that it was obviously not as hard as it had sounded at first. The seed of a potential adventure was now firmly planted in my early teenage mind, but I wasn't quite sure about my ability to ride the distances involved. I knew that France was a small country compared to Australia and therefore the distance to be travelled each day could not be *that* far – after all, riding from one side of France to the other had to be a lot less demanding than trying to do the same thing in Australia.

A month or two earlier our friend Peter and his family had relocated to a newly-developed suburb, and although Tony and I missed his company on our regular bike rides we had managed to stay in touch by phone. Peter had continued to study French at his new high school using the same curriculum, and thus he had been exposed to the same *Tour de France* photos as me. During one of our phone conversations we agreed that during the next school holiday break Tony and I would ride our bikes to Peter's house, stay a couple of nights and then return home. This would be a true test of our ability to ride the *Tour de France* because Peter lived almost 25 miles away!

When the school holidays finally arrived, Tony and I set off for Peter's house at Port Noarlunga one morning with the idea of exploring the limits of our ability. We had never previously ridden more than 5 miles in any one direction, so this was indeed uncharted territory for both of in every sense. Everything went fine for the first 15 miles, at which point we reached the limit of the Adelaide Plains and encountered the base of the first set of hills. We soon concluded that trying to ride up the hill was no fun at all and so instead we dismounted and walked our bikes about a mile-and-a-half to the top of the hill. At this point things became fun again because we were now facing a nice downhill slope. We remounted our bikes and were soon on our way again. This process repeated itself several times until we reached Peter's house and were proud to say that we had covered the distance of 23.4 miles in a little over two hours. These results spoke for themselves and there was no doubt in our minds that we had proved ourselves to be *Tour de France* material.

We did rest for a couple of days before attempting the return journey, but we figured that if we could ride for longer than two hours and cover more than 20 miles in one day then all we would need would be a little bit of practice to get us to ready do the same thing every day for three weeks in France. It all sounded wonderful: by the time we were old enough to go to France and enjoy this two-wheeled holiday known as the *Tour de France* I would have become quite conversant in French, and such a skill might help us meet some French girls. Exactly what we would do when we met said French girls, we weren't quite sure. But we had seen enough television shows and movies to know that it could be interesting to make their acquaintance in between our two hours or so of cycling each day.

I related my *Tour de France* ambitions to my mother upon our return from Peter's house, and although she was not very familiar with France and its culture she had a broad general knowledge that led her to suggest that the bike-riding part of this whole scheme may be quite challenging. I dismissed her motherly concerns with the exasperated air of the well-informed and worldly 13-year-old I considered myself to be when I replied "Well, it's only a bike race. How hard could it be?"

During the following years as I continued to study French under the patient and inspiring Mr. Vale, I maintained a desire to visit France and see for myself the places we had read about in class. Unfortunately the three-man potential Tour de France team disintegrated during this period as Peter had switched from studying French to History, and Tony had left school and started his first job as a bicycle messenger. I couldn't quite understand why, but he swore that last thing he would want to do on a holiday would be to ride a bike.

Meanwhile news of each year's Tour de France was hard to come by in the early 1970s in Australia, with the daily newspaper as the only source of information. The month of July was the height of the football season, and it seemed that the sports editors could seldom find room to report results from a bike race that took place in the middle of the night on the other side of the world. Any news that did appear was in the form of a short list of the overall standings buried in fine print in the back pages of the sport section among the results of the recent pigeon racing and sheaf tossing contests.

After five years of studying French, my enthusiasm to ride in the *Tour de France* had diminished somewhat because by now my primary means of transportation had changed from my trusty Malvern Star bike to a second-hand car. But my desire to visit France had grown considerably, and given the absence of available information to the contrary, at the advanced and sophisticated age of 17 I had no reason to think that the *Tour de France* bicycle race was anything more than an extended vacation on wheels.

It wasn't until 1989 that I was able to visit France for the first time for a tantalizingly brief three-day trip in mid-July by high-speed train from Dieppe to Rouen, on to Dijon and then back to Dieppe to take the ferry back to England. I saw enough of the fleeting scenery during that short trip, and tasted enough of the wonderful food, to know that I must return for a longer period. I was finally able to do so in the mid-90s while working in Sweden, from whence I was able on a number of occasions to take a car ferry to Germany and then drive south to spend a week or two in the rural countryside of Provence.

During the twenty or so years following my first trip to France I returned to Provence on around ten different occasions, and each visit had the effect of making me want to come back again. During the latter part of this period the level of my desire to visit France was further enhanced by the daily telecasts on American television of *Le Tour de France* that constantly showcased verdant and lush countryside interrupted only by charming and picturesque little villages. By this time Lance Armstrong had made quite a name for himself, and even though my main focus was on the scenery I began to notice that the race seemed to call for a level of physical exertion by the riders that was far beyond what my friends and I had imagined in our youth.

Eventually the all-too-close live views of riders climbing impossibly steep mountain roads served to dissolve my romanticized vision of the race. It seemed to be such a wasted opportunity that the riders would be sweating and panting as they followed the bike in front of them instead of proceeding in more leisurely style while admiring the bucolic views that surrounded them on every side. For some 200 riders to take this race-focused, scenery-ignoring approach day after day while travelling to many different parts of France seemed almost criminal to me. And heaven only knows what tasty foods and special wines they were *not* enjoying along the way!

There was only one thing to be done: if those athletes were going to travel around France for three weeks without a single sideways glance or extra helping of dessert, then it was up to me to offer myself as a living example of the correct way to participate in *Le Tour de France*. I would indeed arrange for a three week vacation on wheels – camper van wheels, that is. Instead of having a support team of doctors, psychologists, trainers and masseurs for the journey I would be accompanied by my ever-patient wife. And rather than having the events of each day memorialized in video form, I would use the written word in blog and book form to chronicle my gallant endeavors to enjoy both the race and France itself while supporting the first Australian team to enter the race, Orica-GreenEdge.

I can only hope that you, dear reader, will enjoy reading about my 5,000 kilometer journey to the different corners of France at least half as much as I enjoyed the actual experience!

CHAPTER ONE

BEST LAID PLANS

The best laid schemes of Mice and Men oft go awry,
And leave us nothing but grief and pain,
For promised joy!

ROBERT BURNS

We arrived in Paris on a sunny July day that gave us high hopes for the prevailing weather in the weeks to come. However almost immediately we realized that the attention of the French public at that moment was not focused on Yorkshire where the race was to begin the next day, but instead all eyes were on Brazil and the ongoing FIFA World Cup soccer tournament which was underway. The imagination of the country had been captured by the French national soccer team which was due that evening to play against Germany in a quarter-final match, with the loser eliminated from the tournament. But as may be expected with many things in France that are imbued with multiple layers of meaning, this was to be more than a simple soccer match.

To say that the recent history of "*Les Bleus*" (the Blues), as the French team is affectionately known by its supporters, has been dramatic would be an understatement akin to saying that tennis great John McEnroe was not always in full agreement with the umpire's decisions throughout his career.

At the prior World Cup tournament which took place in South Africa four years earlier, a key player was expelled from the French team as a result of a verbal onslaught directed at the coach. In response to what they perceived as unfair treatment of their discontented colleague, the rest of the team decided to go on strike and refused to leave the team bus after they had arrived for a training session. Disgusted by the whole situation, the team director resigned. Perhaps unsurprisingly given the likely low level of team morale, Les Bleus did not win a game within their group and were quickly eliminated from the tournament.

France has only ever won the world title once, in 1998, but it came close to a second title in 2006 when it narrowly lost to Italy in the final. On the other hand Germany has won the title 3 times, most recently in 1990.

For all of these and many other reasons, I surmised that the atmosphere among the patrons in the bar where I planned to watch the game was likely to be "animated" to say the least, and there was sure to be a very interesting cast of characters on hand. A win by France would create an opportunity for viewing the next match several days later in a different part of France, which would coincide with the first stage of Le Tour on French soil in 2014. One can only imagine the strain placed on sports fans in France on that day, where they would barely have time to squeeze in dinner after watching the closing stretches of Le Tour Stage 4 in Lille before they would be obliged to tune in to Les Bleus playing a semi-final soccer match in Brazil. One could only hope that suitable means of stress relief would be readily available for all concerned, either chilled or at room temperature.

But all of this was in the future. Our first task was to attend to the matter of our rolling holiday home.

Eagerly looking forward to meeting our new best friend the camper van, we engaged a taxi to take us from Charles de Gaulle Airport in Paris to the van rental depot not far from Disneyland Paris in the outer suburbs. When we asked our driver whether he would be watching tonight's World Cup soccer match with France pitted against their archrival Germany, he replied:

"Oh, bien sûr! C'est obligé!"

(Oh, of course! It's compulsory!)

He probably was thinking:

"Crazy foreigners – what a stupid question. Every respectable Frenchman will be watching our brave boys tonight."

Meanwhile we visualized bars, cafés and restaurants full of excited patriots cheering on their gallant lads against all comers. Finally, with strains of the French national anthem *La Marsellaise* playing in my head, we arrived at the camper van depot with plans of joining the crowds of passionate French soccer fans later in the evening to watch the game.

I strode forward into the showroom while mentally patting myself on the back for having used the magic of the internet to organize the perfect van rental from afar. After poring over numerous photographs and drawings of the available rental vehicles I had made my selection of a van that would suit our needs to a tee. Single beds in the back of the van would eliminate the collateral damage caused by the dreaded middle-of-the-night call of nature in a double bed configuration, where one partner would have to crawl over the other to get out of bed while trying not to wake up the crawlee. Meanwhile the crawlee is inevitably woken up but tries their best to go back to sleep knowing full well that a crawl in the opposite direction and being woken up all over again is imminent.

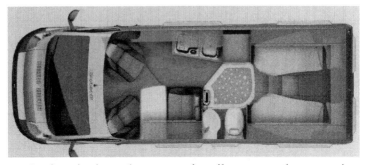

A functioning shower and toilet was also a prime consideration, and the color photographs of these essential items on the rental company's website - together with videos demonstrating the simple ease with which the facilities required for daily ablutions could be set up ready for use – served to flush away any concerns I might have had. A small refrigerator and gas cooktop were also provided and, for good measure I included in my order - at extra cost - a set of kitchen utensils, bedding linen and towels. I had had 9 months or so to plan this trip and wanted to make sure that the camper van that would be the home base, sole form of transportation and hospitality center of our journey would include all the necessary features and comforts including a retractable awning that could be extended to shade us from the hot sun on a lazy afternoon in the countryside.

It soon became clear however, that we were not the only customers that the rental company had to deal with that day.

Several other holidaymakers were returning their campervans at the conclusion of their rental period while others like us were waiting to embark on their extended excursions around France.

We had arrived a couple of hours earlier than our scheduled appointment, which put us into that twilight period of the day before lunch when a Frenchman measures the amount of work awaiting him and compares it to the time available before the immutable noon meal hour. It seemed that there was only one attendant available to take care of processing our rental pick-up, and he quickly surmised that this was a task that could not possibly be accomplished before lunch. In a brilliant stroke of Gallic genius he suggested to us that our problem of having to wait until our scheduled appointment could be solved simply by going to lunch ourselves. He even recommended a suitable restaurant around the corner within walking distance, while confidentially advising us to avoid the nearby pizzeria even though it was a slightly shorter walk.

We of course needed little persuasion to enjoy our first French meal of the trip and set off only to find a rather unpromising looking building displaying the faded advertising signs of what appeared to be a long past heyday. Nevertheless we bravely entered the foyer of the restaurant and were greeted by a trim and smartly dressed couple who might have stepped out of a fashion magazine. Although I warmed to their welcoming attitude, I was sad for this nice couple that their restaurant was silent and deserted at Friday lunchtime which ought to have been one of the busiest meal times of the week. I sighed when the young man showed us into the tastefully-appointed yet empty front part of the dining area but was more than pleasantly surprised when he took us into the next room and the room beyond which were both filled with office workers and business people enjoying the various stages of their lunch.

On any day of the week in a Texas restaurant or Australian pub, unmistakable evidence of the existence of a crowd of this size at lunchtime would be heard loud and clear as soon as the front door was opened. But as seems to be the case throughout France, the contentment of the patrons enjoying good food and company was expressed mainly through their satisfied facial expressions and body language rather than through loud conversation.

We were shown to a table at the back of the restaurant in the fourth part of the dining area which just happened to overlook a tranquil lily pond surrounded by glorious flowers and overhanging shrubs. To think of finding such a setting in an industrial area in the outer suburbs of Paris was difficult enough, but when we reviewed the range of tempting appetizers, main courses and desserts contained within the menus provided to us by the elegantly-dressed hostess, both my wife and I decided that the overnight flight and subsequent taxi ride must have made us delirious. Mindful of the three weeks of dining out ahead of us, we both decided to play it safe and order the *Salade Italienne* which of course we found delicious.

After a satisfying and leisurely lunch we returned to the vehicle depot with eager anticipation to see our new temporary home. After completing the necessary paperwork, the smiling attendant guided us outside so that he could demonstrate the features of the camper van that had been set aside for us.

Although we noticed immediately that it was a different model to the one I had selected on line, it had all of the features that I had expected with two exceptions. There was no retractable awning, and rather than two single beds that could be reconfigured to a double bed if so desired, we found that there was simply a fixed double bed with no scope for reconfiguration. Unfortunately, explained the attendant, the internal configuration with single beds that I had requested was not available and thus the rental company had exercised its contract option to "substitute a vehicle of similar characteristics". Contract options notwithstanding, it was now clear that "night crawler" episodes would be a regular part of our lives for the next few weeks.

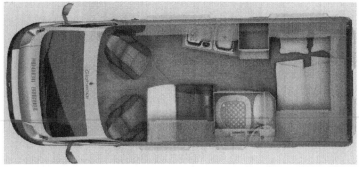

Unless, I thought, we change our sleeping alignment on the bed by 90 degrees so that our feet face the front of the van instead of the side. A quick peek into the back of the van soon made me realize that unless I wanted to sleep in a fetal position for the next three weeks, I was about two feet too tall for this creative new idea to have any prospect of success.

Adding to the irony of the situation, a van with our desired configuration was displayed for sale on the showroom floor at the depot, but alas not for rental. In any case, by the time the attendant had demonstrated all of the van's features to us in a mixture of rapid French and halting English we were quite sure that she would make a comfortable home for the next three weeks. The van was a shiny grey in color with orange paintwork trim that suggested that the vehicle would allow us to roam around the globe at will - perhaps rather optimistically given its apparent lack of airborne or waterborne capabilities. Nevertheless we immediately christened her as "Gisèle the Globetrotter".

We happily drove away with plans to spend our first night in a campground not far from the rental depot where the landscaping feature of a topiary in the shape of the Eiffel Tower at the entrance made it clear that we were "not in Kansas anymore", as Dorothy from the Wizard of Oz might have said.

The decision to stay close to the rental depot that night turned out to be quite fortuitous because as soon as we tried to set up camp in our assigned location we found that a series of problems confronted us: the electric cable provided to us by the rental company was fitted with the incorrect adapter; the gas supply to the cooktop did not work; the electric pump that supplied water to the sink and bathroom was burned out; and even if we did have water for the shower it would not have mattered because the rental depot had not supplied us with any towels.

In other words, on the first night of our long-awaited camper van holiday we had no water, no towels, no gas and no electricity. So much for the "perfect rental" that I had arranged from afar. But while we were reflecting on the state of these inconveniences we learned that we were not alone in lamenting that things had not quite gotten off to the start we might have hoped for.

Orica-GreenEdge Cycling had announced their team for *Le Tour* a couple of days earlier, with the notable omission of the talented South African rider Daryl Impey. Cycling fans initially expressed their outrage via social media that a rider who had led *Le Tour* for two days one year ago was suddenly considered not worthy of selection, but then news emerged that he had been suspended as a result of failing a drug test following a race earlier in the year.

As if this news were not bad enough, the promising young rider Michael Matthews would be unable to participate in *Le Tour* because of injuries he sustained from a crash during a final training ride just prior to leaving to join his teammates for the race. (Two months later it would turn out that Impey's "failed" drug test result was due to an error by the pharmacist and thus Impey had been falsely accused, and was immediately reinstated.)

Although there was nothing we could do for our favorite cycling team, we knew we could address all of our camper van issues the next day at the rental depot. Leaving these concerns behind we turned our attention back to the important matter of the France versus Germany soccer match and walked to the nearby bistro to watch the game and enjoy dinner.

Unlike many sports bars in the US, or hotels in Australia with multiple large television screens, the local bistro near the campground was equipped with only one medium-sized television which looked like it had been borrowed from the owner's living quarters before being plonked unceremoniously on to a low coffee table in the bar area.

An assortment of about ten people of various ages was watching the match in rapt attention when we arrived. A front row of chairs was placed near the screen, with a handful of bar stools arranged haphazardly behind. It soon became apparent that the middle-aged couple in the front row was the bistro's owners, seated alongside their daughter and the daughter's energetic three-year-old son who was clearly not a soccer fan and seemed to have a lot of trouble staying in his chair, much to the consternation of his grandmother.

The game was dominated and eventually won by the German team, and although the atmosphere in the bar was not quite as animated as I had anticipated I was not disappointed in terms of meeting an unusual character or two. Part way through the second half of the game I was approached by a lady of the night who wobbled over and sat right next to me, leaned against my left shoulder, exhaling fumes of some kind of exotic liquor and panting breathlessly in my ear as she asked:

Avez-vous quelqu'une?

(Do you have someone?)

I looked to my right at my wife who was seated next to me and then back at the "lady" who may have been more accurately referred to as a geriatric of the night. I tried as politely as I could to decline her advances and it was only thanks to the help of one of the other patrons that she eventually realized that she would have to look elsewhere to ply her trade.

This incident reminded me of a Saturday morning in Strasbourg some fifteen years earlier when I was out walking to try to find a place to buy a cup of coffee to bring back to my hotel room. That morning I had two encounters with well-dressed young ladies walking on the footpath in the opposite direction to me who both asked me if I had the time. On both occasions I happily replied in my best French that it was five minutes before eight o'clock and then later, ten minutes past eight o'clock. I remembered thinking at the time that it seemed unusual for both young ladies to be dressed for the office so early on a Saturday morning. It was literally several years later when I recounted the incident to an older, well-travelled Swiss acquaintance that I realized I had been subtly invited to enter into a business transaction. And there I had been proudly thinking what a great job I had done to tell them the time in response to their request!

After the game was over, *Madame* the owner tapped us on the shoulder to invite us into the empty dining room where a table for two was set for us. We were surprised to see that we were the only two guests for dinner. In contrast to her earlier stern-faced demeanor when dealing with rowdy customers and a restless three-year-old, she smiled graciously as she brought our appetizer, main course and dessert out to us in stages.

While we were enjoying our dessert, the now well-behaved young grandson helped set ten places at the long table behind us for dinner for *Madame* and her extended family. They soon sat down to eat, and the previously rambunctious youngster was now guided by his parents and grandparents while they shared their meal as a family. We felt honored to be able to discreetly observe the interaction among the members of the family as table manners and traditions were being passed on through the generations by example. Not wanting to disturb the intimate family dinner by asking for our bill, we worked on a conveniently available bottle of *rosé* while they finished their meal. It was at this point that the contented mood within the room was shattered when we discovered the establishment did not accept credit cards.

I was completely surprised at this development since I thought credit cards were accepted everywhere throughout France. Apparently this particular bistro was an exception to the rule. By this time *Madame*'s stern face had returned as she soberly informed me:

"Les panneaux sont partout!"

(The signs are everywhere!)

As I looked around the room and noted the many large signs advertising the bar, different liquors, beers and the World Cup game, Madame pointed out a faded 6-inch-square sign on the wall of the bar showing several credit card symbols crossed out by a thin red letter X. She then took me outside to show me a similarly small sign dwarfed by even larger advertising signs. It seemed clear in her mind that this unfortunate incident was entirely my fault because any imbecile – even a foreigner – would have spotted these easily-noticed signs immediately. I offered to return in the morning with cash but her stern face would have none of it. Perhaps she was feeling a betrayal of trust that she had gone out of her way on our behalf and shared family time with us, only to find that we were now trying to skip out without paying.

I asked where the nearest ATM was located but once again was surprised to learn that it was several miles away in another suburb. By this time it was late on a Saturday evening and after several minutes of discussion it was eventually agreed that I would drive to the ATM in the morning and return with cash. This settlement of the situation was subject to the condition that I leave my driver's license with *Madame* as a security against our enormous debt that tallied up to the grand sum of E46.80 (about $62).

Many things on our first day had not quite turned out as planned, but at least we didn't have to spend our first evening in France washing dishes!

CHAPTER TWO

CASH, CAVALRY AND CALVADOS

Our second day in France began in the same unfortunate style with which the first had ended. A change in the weather had occurred during the night and we awoke to find rain falling on to one end of our bed through the open skylight, creating a small swamp in the quilt. It had been a restless night's sleep in any case as we adjusted to the new time zone and the unaccustomed night crawler arrangements.

A pick-me-up was needed to start the day and we reviewed our options while we lay in bed, carefully avoiding the sodden section. Coffee was out of the question since the gas supply was not working, and even if it had been we would have had to fill the kettle from a garden hose because the van's water pump was also not working. The same constraints prevented us from using the shower in the van, but what about a nice hot shower in the communal ablutions building? That sounded good except for the part about getting dried off afterwards, since we had no towels. We decided that there was only one thing for it, and off we both marched in our bathrobes and sandals with gritted teeth, toiletry kits in hand and an armful of paper towels.

My grandmother used to tell me that a lesson can always be found even in the most difficult of circumstances, and this case was no exception. The lesson to be learned from this particular experience was that the television commercials that tout the wondrous strength and absorption capabilities of kitchen paper towels to clean up common household spills do not always tell the complete truth.

Perhaps things would have been different if I had bathed in a bowl of breakfast cereal or shampooed my hair with tomato sauce, but by the time I had finished trying to dry myself with paper towels that seemed to have the tensile strength of a wet slice of bread and the absorption characteristics of plastic sandwich wrap I looked like I had been dipped in cold water and then rolled in confetti.

Damp little pieces of torn paper were stuck all over me, and I was still wet in many places. But at least the shower had been hot and my bathrobe was able to keep me warm while I slowly dried. My wife's experience with the shower had been very similar to my own, but by gum we were now both well and truly awake and ready for the day!

Why use the artificial stimulant of coffee to wake us up when we have the simple pleasure of a shower and paper towel spa only 50 meters from our doorstep?

Suitably fortified by our adventures in bathing, we dressed and set off to find the nearest automatic teller machine. This journey took us about 5 kilometers away, and even though we were on the outskirts of the Paris suburbs we passed through some pretty green open countryside and flower-lined village boulevards. We would see over the course of the next few weeks that very few open fields nears towns or villages are left uncultivated or allowed to become overgrown with weeds. The corresponding absence of advertising billboards adds to the peaceful ambience of the atmosphere outside the populated areas.

Upon returning to the bistro at around 8 o'clock that morning to pay the bill from the previous night I found the bar populated with a mixed cast of characters of whom several were working on glasses of *rosé* that, judging by the accompanying red noses of the patrons, were likely not their first for the day. Several of the patrons seemed to be farmers who had delivered produce to market early that morning and consequently for whom cocktail hour always arrives early. A few trucks waited outside while their drivers drank what I presumed was coffee from espresso cups, although I suspected some had been reinforced with additional fortification. A couple of tables in a corner were occupied by several rough-looking men, smoking while conversing in low voices and drinking clear liquor, perhaps *marc*, from small glasses.

Perusing this whole scene gave me some insight into the challenges faced by *Madame* the owner as she must deal with customers of all types, keeping her wits about her and taking no nonsense from anyone – especially energetic three-year-old boys and foreigners who can't comprehend the simplest of pictures. I paid the bill and found that *Madame* was much more cordial than she had been late in the prior evening, which I thought was quite an achievement given that she must have risen very early in order to open the bistro for the day at 6am.

With the previous night's debt out of the way and my driver's license recovered, the next step was to drive to the van rental depot to resolve our outstanding problems with Gisèle. We were soon supplied with the correct electric adapter, and the financial manager instructed us to buy towels for which she would later reimburse us. The problem of no gas supply was resolved when one of the attendants showed us a safety valve feature and procedure that had not been explained the day before. This only left the issue of the water pump to be resolved and we were dismayed to be informed that because it was Saturday, there was no technician available to make the repair.

Perhaps the disappointed look on our faces helped, or our explanation that we planned to drive several hundred kilometers to Normandy that day, but in any case the depot supervisor and manager decided to take on the task of replacing the faulty pump. The manager was a slightly older gentleman who did not seem as accustomed to manual labor as his supervisor, but between the two of them they made the repair and by 10.45am we were ready to launch our travelling adventure with Gisèle the Globetrotter.

Our first stop along the way was at a nearby Carrefour supermarket for the purpose of stocking up on supplies for our journey into the distant corners of France. This enormous store could perhaps be described as Walmart on steroids, with the floor space divided about equally between groceries and a department store. However such a comparison does not do full justice to Carrefour.

During the course of our stay in France we visited a number of Carrefour stores and invariably found that the grocery section was a veritable wonderland of fresh vegetables, fruits, meats of all kinds and a wide range of fresh seafood. The dairy shelves were stocked with an enormous range of cheeses and yogurts, and the last couple of rows in the grocery section were devoted to shelf after shelf of wines, spirits and liqueurs. Then there was the bakery with baskets of pastries, baguettes, country-style loaves, croissants and many other kinds of freshly-baked temptations on display.

We ran into a problem when buying a lettuce, however. After the difficult process of selecting which type to buy from among the many on display, we took our selected head to the self-serve scale to weigh it and then print a price label. After scrolling through screen after screen on the computerized scale we could not find the particular variety we had in hand. At this point a young store employee came running toward us, wagging his index finger rapidly back and forth in a manner that resembled the tail of an excitable puppy. At the same time he was saying

Non, non, non! (No, no, no!)

We wondered what we had done wrong and why he was so adamant in his attempt to stop us weighing the lettuce we wanted to buy, but through the use of sign language he indicated that this particular type of lettuce was priced individually and did not need to be weighed. We were grateful to this young man for pointing out this simple error on our part, but we couldn't help but wonder how the same scene would have played out with a French tourist in an American supermarket. I cannot quite imagine that the same level of genuine concern would be so evident on the part of the employee – but then again there would only be a couple of types of lettuce to choose from so making a purchase would likely not be as complicated.

After finishing our grocery shopping, which naturally included stocking up on French wine, we moved to the other end of the store where the first thing we bought was two sets of towels. Dreaming of warm nights in the south of France we considered buying a pair of deck chairs, but left without making a purchase. In any case such dreams or warm summer nights were immediately placed on hold when we walked out of the store into cold and rainy weather.

The rain continued as we drove north to Normandy where we hoped to be able to visit some of the memorials from World War 2. Having read about Normandy and the D-Day landings ever since I was a child, I had long been curious to see the area for myself. There was also a personal connection because Louis, my wife's step-grandfather, had served in the area with the US Army and received a purple heart during the invasion campaign. And Leonard, the father of a good friend of mine had also served with the US Army, and advanced inland with his unit for a number of months after landing in Normandy.

I had first learned of Leonard's service some years ago at a family dinner, when I mentioned how much I enjoyed the apple brandy known as Calvados which is a specialty of the Normandy region. The mention of Calvados triggered a memory for Leonard who informed me that he could not stand its smell or taste.

"I remember one time when my buddies and I were at an empty farmhouse in Normandy" he recounted.

"Our job was to hold that farmhouse and wait for further orders. But the enemy was miles away and so we didn't have much to do, especially at night" he continued.

"What we wanted to do was play cards, but we didn't have a candle to see by. So one of the guys went down into the cellar and found a whole bunch of bottles of Calvados, and that was great for playing cards with."

"Gosh," I replied in what must have been an envious tone "so you had some nice Calvados to enjoy while you played cards?" My mouth practically watered at the thought of this locally-made delicacy fresh from the wine cellar.

"Nah," he replied "ya can't drink that stuff. It's like firewater."

"Well what *did* you do then?" I asked, puzzled.

"We would just open a bottle, put a rag in it and then light it on fire so we could use it as a candle to play cards by." By now I was sorry I had asked the question, and my heart practically bled at the thought of all that lovely Calvados literally going up in smoke.

I had made sure to buy some Calvados on the way to Normandy, but with the memory of Leonard's homespun solution for illumination in mind I made a mental note to keep the precious bottle well away from stray rags, open flames and playing cards.

The rainy weather continued all the way to Normandy where we hoped to be able to see some of the famous beaches where the D-Day landings had taken place. But since it was a holiday weekend in July, it seemed that every other person within a hundred mile radius had the same idea that we did.

Discouraged by the heavy traffic from driving to the beach, we decided instead to set our sights on the town of Le

Havre at the eastern end of the D-Day beaches. However this too turned out to be an unreachable goal because we needed to arrive before the office closed at 8pm at our designated campground, and our late departure from Paris had put us behind schedule.

Reluctantly giving up on our idea of visiting these historic sites, we reset our GPS system to guide us instead to the little seaside town of Veules-les-Roses where our campground awaited. While doing so we gave thanks that the D-Day planners in 1944 had been better organized than we two hapless travelers seventy years later. One can only imagine how the course of history would have been altered if the D-Day armada had decided halfway across the English Channel that they did not have time to land in Normandy as scheduled and instead rearranged their plans to spend the night on one of the Channel islands along the way.

The drive to this little coastal town took us through rolling fields of farmland interspersed with picturesque little villages  where the dominant planting used to form hedges between the houses was the hydrangea shrub. Row after row of green leaves highlighted with large spherical blooms of different shades of pink, lavender, mauve and blue bordered the roadside as we passed through the little villages. Despite the gray and drizzly skies the colors of the flowers stood out like beacons to we two who had so recently left drought-stricken North Texas where a home with even one blooming hydrangea plant in its garden is the envy of all the neighbors.

After checking in at the campground located on a bluff that overlooked the village and which offered an uninterrupted view of the sea, we drove back into the town looking for a restaurant for dinner. Although Gisèle was smaller in size than most of the camper vans we were to see during our journey, at 6 meters (20 feet) in length she was not the easiest vehicle to maneuver through the narrow streets with cars parked on both sides, given also that by this time it was dark and the rain had not stopped. We were about to give up on the idea of trying to find a parking space when a car suddenly pulled out of its parking spot on the side of the street and drove away. We gladly guided Gisèle into the fortuitously-found space and were relieved to find ourselves now parked right in front of *Restaurant La Marine*. This looked like a charming little place with café curtains made from traditional fabric in the windows, and a warm glow of light emanating from within. As we approached the doorway we noted that the credit card logos displayed discreetly near the entrance were satisfyingly devoid of any red X symbols.

Our run of good fortune in finding this little tucked-away restaurant continued throughout the evening as an elderly couple, whom one would think might have less strenuous things to do on a Saturday evening than operate a full-service restaurant, provided wonderful food and service. We both chose escargots for our appetizer, followed by a main course of young chicken roasted in apple cider sauce. Given that the Normandy region is known for producing apples, I naturally followed my meal with a glass of Calvados.

Our culinary experience was similar to that at lunch on the previous day where we had chosen a restaurant at random and on passing through the door found ourselves instantly transported by the ambience of our surroundings, the gracious service of the staff and the sheer quality of the food. It has been my experience throughout my travels in France that much attention is paid to details such as the presentation of food on the plate, and the server will turn the dish as necessary to ensure that the diner's first vision of the plate is exactly as the chef intended. I have often heard the saying from the French that one eats first with one's eyes and such is the custom where all plates at a table are served simultaneously whenever possible, with the aid of multiple servers as needed.

Often the servers will place the plates on the table followed by unveiling their contents with a flourish and a musical-sounding *"Voilà!"* followed by *"Bon appétit, monsieur et madame!"* There is then a collective sharp intake of breath as the diners enjoy both the sight and aroma of the creations placed in front of them, followed a few seconds later by a determined picking up of silverware to get down to the serious business of enjoying the delights prepared for them by the chef.

The pride of the servers in the quality of the food they serve is clearly evident, and for a diner to simply pick up a knife and fork and start eating before taking a few moments to admire the chef's handiwork set out on the plate would be seen as either an insult to the establishment or as evidence of complete ignorance of dining etiquette.

In another parallel to the previous day, we found ourselves next to a large table with three generations of a family enjoying their meal together, with the grandparents gently guiding the children with their table manners.

Sigmund Freud may have famously said that "Sometimes a cigar is just a cigar", but in France a restaurant meal is almost always more than a meal: it is both a culinary and cultural experience.

CHAPTER THREE

STACCATO SHOWERS AND SEQUENTIAL SNACKBARS

The rain continued through the night but by now we had not only learned to look for credit card signs, we had also learned to close the skylights of the van before retiring.

The next morning was Sunday and we were eager to attend Mass in the beautiful old stone church that we had driven past in the village. We were to find that the church of St. Martin dates from the 13th century, but alas we were also to learn that the building is now used as a museum rather than an operating church. Unable to find evidence on the internet of any other active churches nearby we enjoyed a leisurely morning. Well, mostly leisurely except for the shower arrangements.

Of course we now had the luxury of towels made of spun cotton instead of paper, but we had decided that even though the luxury of hot running water was also now available in the van the thought of confining oneself to a shower enclosure the size of a telephone booth suitable only for an anorexic chimpanzee was entirely unappealing. Once again donning our bathrobes and sandals we trekked across to the communal bathing block, clutching our toiletry kit, towel, toilet paper and soap.

Having grown up in the driest capital city in the driest continent on earth, I am all for water conservation. Allow me to make it clear that I am far more conscientious about turning off taps and saving water than most people I have met in the United States. But I am at a loss to understand why the flow of water in the showers in the campground bathing block would cut off after 15 seconds, especially given the fact that we just had endured almost 24 continuous hours of rain with more on the way.

This parsimonious shower scheme caused a typical series of events that can best be described as follows. I step into the shower cubicle, remove my robe and hang it on the hook provided. Turning to the shower I press the button that is located where a tap (or even two taps) would normally be located in a more lugubrious locale. A thin stream of cold water squirts out from a shower nozzle mounted near the ceiling, and while I'm still looking to find out how to adjust the temperature to a less frigid temperature the flow of water drizzles to a stop. Fully 15 seconds have elapsed, my brief ration of water has ended for the time being and I have been sprinkled by just enough cold water to make me shiver but not quite enough to make a lather for any useful purpose.

Starting again, I press the button and adjust a nearby control knob that seems to imply that it knows where to find some warmer water. Just as the water does indeed transition from the Arctic to a more mid-Atlantic temperature, my strict ration of 15 seconds expires.

I now realize that each 15-second burst of activity should be planned in advance, and I begin by standing on my tiptoes to adjust the direction of the nozzle. While smugly thinking to myself that only someone with my height in excess of six feet could work the system to his advantage by adjusting the shower nozzle I quickly find out that I am outsmarted by a nozzle that refuses to move. Meanwhile a chill is returning to my body as the lukewarm water all over me is now feeling decidedly cold.

Admitting defeat I now start to rush through a staccato series of 15 second bursts of frenzied activity with soap and shampoo, which all go as well as can be expected until the water cuts out while I have shampoo in my eyes and can't see to find the button to restart the flow. In my fumbling foray I do manage to find the control that switches the water back to cold and so when I eventually restart the water flow I find myself instantly transported from the Caribbean to the Antarctic. It was no wonder that I was exhausted by the time I had finished my shower – after all, I had travelled from one end of the world to the other.

My wife reported that her shower experience was about as relaxing as mine had been but with the added minor complication that she dropped the soap and had to reach blindly under the wall of her shower stall into the next cubicle to recover it, fervently hoping that it was unoccupied at the time.

With all of this excitement to occupy us, we lost track of the time and by the time we were ready to leave the campground we found it was ten minutes past the appointed noon check-out hour. I knocked on the closed office door and in due course a stern young man appeared, told me to come back at 2pm, and closed the door again. I was momentarily stunned by this lack of flexibility on his part until I realized that I had intruded on the sanctity of the lunch hour. What on earth had I been thinking when I tried to get him to take 5 minutes out of his preciously-short two hour lunch break to take back my gate key, punch a few numbers into his computer and give me a receipt? I hoped he would have forgiven my impertinence by the time we were to meet again after lunch.

Meanwhile we set off to explore the local area which we found was in the midst of its annual festival celebrating linen and hand-embroidered needlework. On the way to Veules-les-Roses the previous day we had passed numerous fields planted in the flax plants from which linen is made, and we saw many more as we drove between the neighboring villages which were also celebrating the festival. The countryside itself was a patchwork of colors with pale green fields of flax, brown fields of wheat and dark green fields of potatoes. Cattle of a mixture of colors roamed in green pastures set against the backdrop of the pale blue-grey sea while hydrangeas of many shades punctuated the village streets along with colorful festival banners bravely trying to defy the persistent wind and rain that threatened to spoil many of the planned outdoor events. The *Tour de France* had started the day before in England and we pitied the riders battling what must have been windy and rainy conditions similar to those we were experiencing in France.

At one point we drove along a lovely seafront esplanade area and were pleased to see several roadside stalls advertising fresh seafood. We pulled over, eagerly anticipating a taste of fresh oysters and other local delicacies. However Fate must have decided that it needed to reinforce the lesson that it was trying to teach me, because all of the stalls were closed for lunch. If Logic were to take a hand in this discussion it might point out the absurdity of a vendor closing his business expressly at the time that it is most likely to receive the most customers. In any case the point had been made: a Frenchman's lunch break is sacrosanct and this rule must never be violated. (Cue wagging index finger for emphasis.)

As we entered the quaint little village of St Aubin-sur-mer  we encountered a beautiful old stone church and were pleased to see its front door open. With our hopes buoyed that we could attend Mass we entered and found that although this church from the 17th century looked as though it were still the home of an active congregation, on this festival weekend it was the home of an extensive and very impressive display of embroidered linen.

After finally checking out at our campground from the previous night we headed towards Amiens, which we hoped would give us an opportunity to visit some of the historic sites of World War 1.

While checking in at our campground in Amiens we asked the

clerk for a recommendation for a nearby restaurant, preferably within walking distance. There was nothing close by, but he recommended a couple of places in the city while warning us that the streets were narrow. He then mentioned that the campground had its own "snackbar". We visualized the unappealing prospect of a small storefront selling chips and soft drinks, but the prospect of navigating Gisèle through the narrow streets of a medieval town was equally unappealing. After deciding to stay put we were happily surprised to find that the "snackbar" was in fact a pleasant little café with a full bar, beer on tap and a range of liqueurs. The enterprise was operated by a middle-aged man who acted at once as waiter, bartender and chef. This solo staffing situation meant that service was offered in sequential fashion rather than parallel. That is to say instead of working on several tables at the same time, the hard-working Jacques-of-all-trades served his clientele by taking the orders from one table, then cooking and serving those meals before moving on to take orders from the next table to start the process all over again. Fortunately there were only four occupied tables, and thankfully he managed to at least serve drinks in parallel fashion which kept the customers happy while we all waited with bated breath to see which table would be next to win the honor of being allowed to order meals.

The menu was limited to a choice between *coq au vin* (chicken in red wine) and *bayard de veau* (tender chunks of veal in mushroom sauce); with both dishes accompanied by a copious amount of frozen *pommes frites* (french fries) in lieu of any other kind of vegetable. Not that anyone would have complained about the lack of any other vegetables or that the potatoes were mass-produced: I think I speak for all of my fellow snackbar patrons from that evening when I say that the thought of watching potatoes being peeled, sliced, parboiled and then sautéed in sequence for one table after another would have been enough to make us throw ourselves under the nearest passing camper van.

Apart from the spectacle of watching the manifestation of the proprietor's customer service tunnel vision, we were also kept entertained by the television tuned to the finish of an important World Cup soccer match, followed by the final set of the Men's Singles Final at Wimbledon. During the tennis it became clear from overheard exclamations and snatches of conversation that that the customers at the other three tables in the café were all from Great Britain, thereby presenting the ideal opportunity for me to test my "moustache theory".

Much to the probable, but graciously unexpressed, annoyance of my wife I had been studiously cultivating my moustache for the previous few months leading up to *Le Tour*. My goal was to use this facial camouflage to make me appear as if I were French, which I thought was quite a plausible plan since many Frenchmen of my certain age possess a large and carefully unkempt decoration of this type on their upper lip.

The purpose of wanting to appear French was strictly journalistic in nature: I wanted to be able to hear what English-speaking people say about their surroundings in France when they think that no-one can understand them. Of course it would be one thing to *look* French, but to complete the ruse I would also have to make sure to speak with the staff throughout the evening only in French. And when speaking in English to my wife - who does not speak French - I would have to ensure that no neighboring tables could overhear us.

Strict self-discipline on my part over several hours would be required to pull off this marvelous social experiment that would allow me to see how others see France and its people. It could indeed be the genesis of a whole new series of scholarly sociological essays and perhaps eventually lead to a Ph.D. thesis of unique character: "Uncensored Insights Into The French Experience From An Unconscious Anglophone Perspective".

Astute readers will by now have deduced that the circumstances of this particular setting in which I was drinking wine on an empty stomach while surrounded by English families watching tennis from Wimbledon were not conducive to achieving the longed-for results I had in mind. I'm not quite sure what gave me away - whether it was occasionally laughing at the humorous comments about the tennis made by the Liverpudlian father at the next table, commenting loudly in English at a bad call by a tennis line judge, or reading a received text on my phone out loud to my wife – but somehow I received no ground-breaking insights that night, unconscious or otherwise. It also didn't help that I was also so intent on eating my long-awaited dinner and watching the tennis that I entirely forgot to pay close attention to the conversations of the other tables.

It looks like my Ph.D. will have to wait, although that's not such a bad thing because it will likely take a while for the world to come to terms with my special method of data-gathering that some unenlightened and unscholarly folks might regard as eavesdropping. I guess I'm just a man ahead of his time, even if my wife tends to think the exact opposite when looking at my moustache.

CHAPTER FOUR

FAMILY CONNECTIONS

The next day began with a staccato shower followed by another trip to Carrefour to buy the remainder of the essentials for our trip and groceries for the next few days. By now we were becoming familiar with the strictly-enforced rules of access to a Carrefour store, in which one may only enter through the solitary lane for this purpose which is invariably placed at one end of the store, but may exit through any of the almost innumerable checkout lanes. A casual observer may think it strange that patrons must literally go out of their way to follow such a closely-monitored process to enter the store. Indeed we had learned our lesson after being confronted on several occasions with a metronomic index finger while trying to enter the store via an empty checkout lane, only to be forced to walk to the other end of the store to enter through the sacred *Entrée* (Entrance) portal.

Upon thinking this through, the reason for what at first glance seems like a strange approach to store security is in reality rather obvious. In many parts of the world, entry to a retail store is freely available but the exit process is strictly controlled to avoid the possible theft of goods by customers.

Anyone exiting a store must pass by a cashier and pay for the goods they have with them or else leave the store empty-handed. However at Carrefour in France, as we have seen, the system is quite the opposite in that customer *entry* is controlled but customer *exit* is not.

The inescapable conclusion is that the esteemed management of the Carrefour Corporation is guarding against the possibility that customers may attempt to enter the store and bring goods with them. The purpose of the single entrance lane therefore is to ensure that all customers enter the store empty-handed and don't attempt to smuggle any outside products in with them. In other words while stores in many other places work hard to avoid shop*lifting*, the guardians of Carrefour in France are doing their level best to eradicate the scourge of shop*dropping*.

Our next stop was the town of Houplines on the outskirts of Lille in northeast France, where Stage 4 of *Le Tour* was due to finish the next day. This was to be the first stage on French soil after the first three stages had taken place under rainy conditions in England. After a couple of hours on the road after leaving Amiens, and just as I was mentally congratulating myself on planning the itinerary to bring us to the starting point of the race in good time, my wife did some quick research on her phone and found that we had left behind us unseen the spectacular Gothic cathedral of the Basilica of Our Lady of Amiens.

A little advance research on my part would have allowed us to make time to see the tallest complete cathedral in France, built between 1220 and 1270. But we did have a plan to make a stop on the way to Houplines to visit the grave of my great-great-uncle George F. Banner who died in the

Pozières campaign which was part of the Battle of the Somme during World War 1.

George was a farm laborer from rural Victoria who had enlisted on August 31st, 1915 at the age of 23. After completing his periods of training in Australia and Egypt, Private Banner landed in Marseilles on March 26, 1916 and was part of the 8th reinforcements for the 23rd Battalion of the 1st Division of the Australian Imperial Forces. According to his official service record George first saw action on the night of June 29th when he "took part in a raid on the enemy's trenches". He was wounded in action one month later on July 27th during the battles surrounding the village of Pozières and died of his wounds the next day. He was buried in the "British Cemetery Bapaume Post on the Albert-Bapaume road 1¼ miles N.E. of Albert".

As was not uncommon in the confusion of battle, communication of information from the front was sporadic and unreliable. Consequently his parents were informed of George being wounded on July 27th but did not receive news of his death until some months later. In the meantime they received a letter from one of their two other sons who were also serving in France, in which my great-grandfather Clifford informed his parents that he had heard news from his comrades of the death of his brother George.

The battle of Pozières lasted two weeks and the number of casualties on both sides was enormous. According to the official records the 23rd Battalion sustained a 90% casualty rate during the Pozières campaign. And having just received reinforcements to bring it close to its full complement of 1,023 men, it's little wonder that the Australian official historian wrote that the Pozières ridge "is more densely sown with Australian sacrifice than any other place on earth".

With this brief history in mind we arrived at a British cemetery south of Pozières in which 300 Australian graves

were included among the rows of fallen British and Canadian soldiers. The cemetery itself was immaculate, surrounded by granite walls and entered through an imposing archway. The grass between the rows of graves was neatly maintained, and the headstones were each engraved with military insignia in addition to the details of the deceased. In all it was a comfortingly tranquil scene that belied the loud and savage violence that had taken place in the area 100 years earlier.

Between the two of us, my wife and I read every headstone in the cemetery but did not find the one we were looking for. During the midst of our search an older couple arrived and offered to help us look for George F. Banner. John and his wife were visiting from the Netherlands and they showed us where to find the reference book that is kept near the entrance gates. This book listed the names and locations of all of the men buried in the cemetery, but alas my great-great-uncle was not among them. It was very kind of them to offer to help but we now  understood that we were in the wrong cemetery. My wife and I were just about out of time to search any further, but the Dutch couple planned to visit a few more cemeteries that day and offered to keep an eye out for my "old uncle", as John referred to him.

Turning the conversation to lighter matters, we learned that they too were going to watch *Le Tour*. John was gleefully looking forward to Stage 5 which was scheduled for two days hence along a route that would include some 13 kilometers of cobblestones. He positively glowed with anticipation at the chaos that might erupt among the riders on that day, rubbing his hands together with joy.

Shortly after resuming our drive towards the campground at Houplines we found another British cemetery with many Australian graves included. Consulting the reference book we found that my great-great-uncle was not among the interred in this location. By this time it was too late to search further so we resolved to add a Pozières exploration to a Normandy exploration on our next trip.

We drove on through more beautiful countryside interspersed with crops of wheat, potatoes, corn, and lettuce. Even though the crops varied from one field to the next, almost all of the fields seemed to have a sprinkling of red poppies around the edges that created a poignant reminder of the blood spilled in those French fields by men from many countries of the world.

We arrived at our campground in Houplines – near Lille -  just before dusk and enjoyed a nice dinner that my wife cooked in the van using chicken breast and salad that seemed so much more flavorful than we were accustomed to tasting in Texas. Meanwhile the colorful circus and caravan known as *Le Tour de France* was due to cross the English Channel that evening for the commencement of the fourth of 21 stages of this year's event. After the first three stages had taken place in England in front of enormous crowds who braved the rainy weather, the separation between the leaders and a number of other contenders was only two seconds. The race leader at this point was the Italian rider Vincenzo Nibali, but Michael Albasini from Orica-GreenEdge was one of the twenty riders placed only two seconds behind the leader. Given that the riders had already spent more than 13 hours on their machines and the total duration of the race was likely to be in the region of 90 hours, a two second margin was quite inconsequential and indicated potentially exciting times ahead as riders would seek to distance themselves from their competitors in the coming days.

Just before the fading light at our campground made it too dark to see, a group of four young adults arrived in a car and set up a tent in the lot next to us, from which we were separated by a hedge. As soon as the tent was up they strung up a clothes line and hung wet clothes out to dry. Almost immediately it began to rain, and my wife noticed a mosquito inside the van. Little did we realize how much these two seemingly innocuous events would shape our next few days.

CHAPTER FIVE

GREYHOUNDS ON BIKES

The overnight continuation of the rainy weather that had prevailed since our arrival in France did nothing to dampen our enthusiasm for the first stage of the 2014 *Tour de France* to take place on French soil. However the same could not be said for the tent-dwellers in the lot next to us. Looking out through the window of our van I could see that their garments on the clothes line were now wetter than they had been the night before. In addition we noted that they had pitched their tent in the lowest point in their appointed space, and as a result the tent was sitting in what was by now a shallow pool of water. There was no sign of movement from within the tent, so we could only assume that the waterproof floor of the tent had done its job of keeping the occupants safe and dry. Either that or all 4 of the occupants were gently floating on their airbeds inside the tent, blissfully oblivious to the rising waters below them.

Our alarm had seemed to sound much earlier than its appointed time of 7.30am, but that was probably because we had slept so soundly with the soothing patter of rain on the roof of the camper van through most of the night. After walking over to the common facility we found that the showers at this particular campground were the most generous that we had experienced so far, offering a positively extravagant 30 seconds of hot water with each press of the control button. But this luxury did not come without a price: there was no source of light in the shower stall. However a single light fixture in the room spilled over the top of the stall and provided a dim glow to help proceedings along. Luckily by now I know where most of my bodily extremities are located and can reliably reach most of them without the necessity of ambient lighting.

With our adventures in ablutions behind us, we set off for the race with the hope of finding a place on an uphill stretch of the route where the riders would be travelling more slowly and could more readily be seen. We arrived at the race route at 9am and found that even at that relatively early hour there were already a number of campers, cars and caravans parked alongside the road despite the continuing drizzle. Knowing that the uphill vantage points would be more popular and thus likely fully occupied by now, we parked our van on a flat stretch of road about 21 kilometers (13 miles) from the finish line fully aware that the first riders were not scheduled to pass by until about eight hours later.

While we awaited the arrival of Le Tour we used our spare time wisely with a breakfast prepared in the camper consisting of free-range eggs sautéed in olive oil and served on crusty French bread, accompanied by espresso coffee and organic yogurt.

Just as with a number of other food items that we had already encountered during our journey thus far, the eggs that we had bought from the supermarket were bursting with flavor – even though persuading each individual egg to "burst" out of its shell was not a quest for the timid or faint-hearted soul. The shells of these locally-produced eggs were more robust than any that we had ever encountered.

It took my wife several progressively harder blows on the side of the frypan before she could induce any sign of a blemish in the first egg she attempted to crack. Finally she had to hold the pan with one hand and hit the egg against the edge with the other before she was able to crack the egg sufficiently to allow the contents to ooze their way into the pan. This in itself was a revelation because the yolk was almost orange in color, a far cry from the pale lemon-colored yolks that we have been accustomed to seeing in the eggs purchased from our local supermarkets in the United States. Needless to say, the hard-won contents of the eggs provided a delicious start to our day.

But all of this exertion cracking Hercules-like eggs and chewing crusty bread was very tiring and thus a nap was called for as soon as the dishes were cleared away. Unable to resist the siren call, we retired to the opposite end of the van for a cozy 90-minute nap surrounded by the gentle sounds of the rain continuing to fall.

With time to spare after our mid-morning snooze, we walked along the route into the nearest town, Capinghem. During the previous few days we had enjoyed several daily workouts that involved raising glasses and lifting food to our mouths but this this was the first significant physical activity to involve our legs since we had arrived in France.

Along the way we passed through a residential area in which many otherwise ordinary-looking houses had been rendered quite charming in appearance through the strategic use of flowering window boxes and shrubbery, including of course the ever-present hydrangeas with which we had by now become fascinated.

As we came closer to the center of the small town, we passed a home with shuttered windows opening directly on to the street. Upon passing the open kitchen window we found ourselves almost within arms-length of a large family seated around a table enjoying their lunch. This was a scene we would see repeated throughout our journey, with friends and families gathered to enjoy a convivial lunch before the arrival of *Le Tour*.

The entire race takes place on public roads which must be temporarily closed to other traffic to allow free passage of the bike riders and their support vehicles. This presents quite a logistical challenge to the organizers since several of the 21 stages are in excess of 200 kilometers (125 miles) in length. A great deal of manpower is required to close the roads a few hours in advance of the riders and stop misguided tourists or over-exuberant spectators from straying in to the path of the race.

On the rainy day of Stage 4, gendarmes lined the route through Capinghem streets at 400 yard intervals, politely enforcing the road closure and patiently explaining the situation to frustrated local residents who wanted to drive out of their streets to perhaps buy provisions for lunch but found their path barred. By about 1pm the road was deserted and almost silent except for the sounds of ongoing pre-race lunches and related celebrations from the various cars and camper vans spaced at intervals along the road.

Most vehicles displayed the allegiance of their owner in one form or another such as a national flag or a banner with the name of a favorite team or individual rider, but the level of socializing between spectators was curtailed by the heavy rain showers that passed by periodically.

Opposite us was a grandfather from Belgium who had towed from across the nearby border an almost microscopic two-wheeled camper trailer complete with a pair of regular-sized grandchildren. A large Belgian flag occupied most of one side of the trailer, obscuring one of the windows so that the  grandchildren were obliged to take it in turns to pop their head into the rain through the doorway to look up the road for the first signs of the approaching race.

The showers eventually ceased but the weather remained overcast, cool and damp for the eagerly-awaited arrival of the Publicity Caravan. While spectators sitting safely out of the rain watching the race on television could expect to be subjected to advertising at regular intervals, even the cycling fans who watch the race in person do not escape the long reach of advertising. Some 90 minutes before the riders pass a given point on each day's route, a series of floats and trucks passes by advertising the wares of the sponsors of the race while throwing out small giveaway items to the spectators gathered on the side of the road. On this particular day the Caravan arrived slightly late, clearly having been delayed in its progress by the rain. When it passed by our position the vehicles were travelling in quite a hurry, trying to make up time.

Several trucks sponsored by PMU drove past, playing loud dance music. On the back platform of each truck were two young ladies gamely trying to dance, wearing yellow rain ponchos and forced smiles against the cold and damp. The array of floats was very creative, including several that featured a person sitting in a chair or on the saddle of a horse or bicycle. In each case, those poor souls seated facing the wind seemed to look like they would rather be somewhere else instead of being strapped into a stationary position while being exposed to the elements on the back of a fast-moving vehicle.

After the Caravan had passed, a number of families who had arrived on foot left for home. This was a scene we would see repeated throughout our journey as excited children waited for the arrival of the Caravan, gathered up as many small prizes as they could and then set off for home. Many of these families were replaced by adult spectators from the local region who arrived on foot after the passing of the Caravan to get down to the serious business of watching the race.

We had been waiting since 9am and when the riders came by just after 5pm they seemed to pass more quickly than a fleeting shower on a spring day. Within the space of 60 seconds they had arrived with a rush and great intensity, and very quickly they were gone. The French rider Thomas Voeckler was in the lead, having sprinted away from the pack early in the stage. When he passed us he was still about 20 seconds ahead and he looked like a rabbit running from a pack of pursuing dogs. Indeed all of the riders looked lean and fit, reminding me of a pack of greyhounds as they swished by in flurry of multiple colors. It was another 5 kilometers before the pack caught up with Voeckler and left him in their wake after he had held the lead for more than 140 kilometers (88 miles).

Talking about the events of the day, Voeckler was quoted after the race: "I wanted to blow the dust off my engine. I'm 35 years old and a diesel, so it takes a while to warm up". Despite his brave efforts, he was the 178th rider to cross the finish line among the 194 who completed the stage. Losing almost 5 minutes of time overall hardly seemed like a just reward for a man who had worked so hard for most of the stage, however it spoke volumes about the levels of athleticism and determination that are required to compete in *Le Tour de France*.

After the riders had passed by we decided to join the celebrations in town. The lunch hour had exhibited quite a festive atmosphere and we assumed that the dinner hour would comprise a continuation of the day's festivities. We recalled having seen an intriguing restaurant on our walk earlier in the day, and now that the roads were clear we drove into town to *La Mère Simone*. This restaurant was located in a charming two-story house that looked like it had been converted for the purpose. We arrived just before 6pm and found that the tastefully-decorated main dining room was almost empty, which I took to mean that we had managed to arrive before the post-race rush. However after serving us a drink the owner informed us that the restaurant had been open all afternoon and would close at 6.30pm. Disappointed, we finished our drinks and left in search of another alternative in the town.

But we soon found that the crowds had disappeared and the streets were quite empty. Pizza was not necessarily what we had in mind for dinner on the evening of our first stage of

Le Tour, but it was the only available option and we enjoyed the experience of being served by a young man who regarded his establishment as a restaurant rather than a fast food operation and treated his customers accordingly. Once again we detected a sense of pride and teamwork in which the waiter's role was to ensure that we understood what we were ordering and were happy with the results. This type of service mentality stands in sharp contrast to many less formal restaurants in the United States where the waiter seems to see his or her role as totally separate from the kitchen, and the only reason to offer good service is to increase the chances of receiving a good tip. But on the other hand, who can blame the American waiters who often are paid only a few dollars per hour and are forced to rely on tips to make up the difference in comparison with their French counterparts who are paid a more generous hourly rate?

After a relaxed meal during which we realized we could not single-handedly resolve the differences between the French and American economic systems we decided it was time to return to the campground and retire for the night.

We would need our wits about us because tomorrow promised to be an action-packed day. This was to be the stage in which the Tour riders would navigate a number of sections of cobblestones. We imagined that our new Dutch friend John would be positively salivating in anticipation.

What is the Publicity Caravan and what does it have to do with a bike race?

It takes a lot of money to support the logistics of staging *Le Tour de France* each year, with its 198 riders travelling over 3,500 km around France in the space of 23 days. By the same token, hundreds of thousands of people in France come out to watch at least part of each day's stage, thereby offering an attractive opportunity for advertisers to gain publicity.

The net result is that a small of companies or organizations sponsor the Tour in return for being able to advertise their products and services to the crowds that line the route for each of the 21 stages. They do so in the form of a "Publicity Caravan" which is a parade of floats and vehicles that travel the route of each day's stage at slow speed about 90 minutes before the riders pass by.

Free product samples are thrown from the floats and eagerly gathered by the spectators, mostly the children. In fact many families who have small children come to the race route especially for the Caravan and then go home with happy youngsters with loot in hand. The Caravan is never seen on TV outside France because its message is aimed at consumers in France, and not elsewhere.

Here is some information by the numbers about the 2014 Publicity Caravan.

180: The number of vehicles that make up the Caravan each day, which includes 15 vehicles from the local Press in the region that *Le Tour* is traversing on that particular day.

12: The length of the Caravan in kilometers (7.5 miles), which advertises to millions of people on the side of the road every year in an event that takes 35-40 minutes each day to pass a given point.

600: The number of people who work on the vehicles in the Caravan each day.

CHAPTER SIX

UNDAMPENED ENTHUSIASM

On our return to the campground the previous evening we had found that our tent neighbors had relocated overnight to a higher part of their allotment after discovering that water flowed unrelentingly downhill into the hollow where they had originally pitched their tent. This was just as well because the rain continued overnight, dampening everything except the enthusiasm of the local mosquitoes.

I can make this statement about the mosquito population with authority because I had brought with me the most reliable barometer of mosquito activity known to man – my wife. Over the past number of years that we have lived in Texas she has demonstrated the extent of her insect-attracting skills time and again, even in the most unlikely of settings where one would not expect to encounter such creatures. No matter the time of day it seems that any stray mosquito within flying distance is inexorably drawn to my wife's bare flesh, no matter how little of such flesh may be exposed at the time. And on early evening occasions when we are sitting outside in the backyard enjoying a glass of wine with a meal from the barbecue, she will find herself positively swarmed with unsolicited airborne admirers while I'm sitting next to her, untouched and obliviously unaware of any flying pests.

Even though the temperature in north-east France was quite cool at the time that we visited, it seems that the earlier days of summer had seen the hatching of a healthy population of mosquitoes who apparently held no objection to enjoying an American diet. In her turn, my wife rewarded their efforts with an array of small red lumps that gradually increased in size and number over the next few days.

After studying the day's route for Stage 5, we chose a location near Pont Thibault which was on one of the cobblestoned sections of the route. Our motivation was not to watch riders falling in the difficult conditions, but rather to get a better look at the riders who would likely be travelling more slowly under the difficult conditions. Our Dutch friend John must have been delighted because the rain was very heavy and the nine sections of cobblestone on the route would be particularly difficult to manage, especially since these sections of road were narrow and the riders would likely be bunched together as they wobbled their way along. As it turned out, we later learned that the organizers of the race decided to remove two of the scheduled nine sections of cobblestones from the route in recognition of the dangers involved.

Even though it was raining when we set off, nothing could diminish the beauty of the countryside we drove through on the way to watch *Le Tour*. One may think to explain the unexpected attractiveness by saying that this particular part of France is different because it has agricultural areas close to the large towns, but the more I saw of the country the more I realized that fields of cattle, sheep, wheat, corn, potatoes, cabbage and onions can be seen in any space where the available land allows. This in turn is evidence of the French connection to food and the freshness of the produce that forms the basis of the national diet.

As a small example of how this concept is carried through to everyday life, one might stop at a regular gas station on the side of the road with the thought of picking up a sandwich for lunch while driving to one's destination. Instead of finding a label on the wrapping that shows that the sandwich should be eaten on or before a date 3 or more days from now, in France one would find that the expiry is expressed as a time in minutes and hours later on that very same day of purchase. In other words there is no reason not to munch on a fresh sandwich while waiting for the weather or traffic to clear, and the range of available ingredients ensures that even a blindfolded selection will seldom disappoint.

By the time we arrived at our chosen destination and parked on a country road surrounded by miles of crops in each direction, we found that there were already a number of vans, cars and campers in position along the nearby cobblestone section. As was the case the previous day there was a strong presence from Belgium but also there were a number of British flags and fans supporting the prior year's winner Chris Froome. Learning from the experience of the previous day, we parked Gisèle on the left side of the road facing the oncoming riders whom we would see approaching through the windscreen. This would allow us to remain warm and dry inside the van until the last possible moment when we would exit the van to cheer on our favorites.

Meanwhile it was time for a breakfast of sardines in tomato sauce served on French bread, accompanied by espresso coffee and yogurt. In recognition of the fact that the volume of product derived from an espresso coffee maker is relatively small in comparison with the volume of hot liquids we were accustomed to consuming during a typical day, we had stopped along the way to buy instant coffee to supplement the espresso. During a brief lull in the weather after breakfast my wife walked to a nearby supermarket about 10 minutes distant to buy larger coffee cups and a few other items.

While trying to check out with her purchases she tried to explain to the cashier that the US credit card she was using needed to be swiped through the merchant's card reader and then validated with a signature. This was in contrast to the European system in which credit cards are embedded with a microchip and are read simply by inserting the card into a slot provided on the merchant's card reader.

The line behind her started to grow as my wife tried in vain to explain the difference in card usage to the cashier. The fact that my wife speaks no French did not help the situation, and the resulting financial impasse might have continued for some time except for the kindness of the French lady in front of her who offered to help, eventually guiding the transaction to a successful conclusion. My wife thanked her benefactor with a mixture of sign language and a few simple words before taking her leave to walk back to the van.

The heavy rain had resumed while my wife was in the store and when she was about halfway back to the van a car pulled up alongside her. It was the same helpful lady from the checkout line who emerged from her vehicle and although she spoke no English managed to communicate an offer to drive my wife back to our van. The offer was very gratefully accepted and my wife was returned to the van safely and not quite as wet as would otherwise have been the case. Who said French people are rude?

As was expected by all – and eagerly anticipated by others – Stage 5 of *Le Tour* was very difficult in windy, rainy, cold conditions, with cobblestones making life even more unpleasant for the riders. In fact the conditions were so bad that the entire Publicity Caravan was cancelled for the day, much to the disappointment of my wife who had hoped to nab one of the colorful Carrefour tablecloths we had seen the day before.

When the riders arrived at our location, having just traversed the second cobblestone section of the day, they were led by a breakaway group of seven riders that included Simon Clarke and Mat Hayman from the Orica-GreenEdge team. This small group was about two minutes ahead of the rest of the pack and each rider looked clean and calm. In stark contrast to the previous day when the remaining riders resembled a large pack of greyhounds, today they were spread out and resembled a pack of worn-out, discouraged and muddy terriers that had been chasing rabbits all over a wet field and had so far come up empty-handed.

This was a day that illustrated how challenging *Le Tour* really can be for those who join the fray. The riders in the main group (commonly called the "peleton") looked cold and miserable. By the time the riders passed our position, numerous among them had already fallen, and last year's winner and this year's favorite Chris Froome had fallen twice and dropped out of the race entirely. The two falls would later be found to have caused fractured bones in Froome's left wrist and right hand.

While the numerous British supporters on hand would have been sorely disappointed by the news, supporters of the overall race leader Vincenzo Nibali would have been pleased that he not only survived the day intact but also distanced himself further from his challengers. Spanish rider Alberto Contador who had been expected to contend for the overall win of the race lost time due not only to the difficult conditions but also due to mud that had jammed some of the gears on his bike, thus hampering his ability to maintain the necessary pace. Meanwhile Mat Hayman and Simon Clarke saw their early lead in the stage fade away, and they finished 12th and 50th respectively on the day.

On our way back to our campground – or "the mosquito swamp", as my wife was already calling it – we kept an eye out for an ATM, hoping that such conveniences would be more prevalent than had been the case in the outer suburbs of Paris. While passing through La Chapelle d'Armentières we spotted a bank near the large roundabout at the center of the town. After parking across the street I hopefully walked over and found to my amazement that the branch was still open at 6.45pm on a Wednesday evening. One of the employees greeted me cheerfully as I walked in, but all I could do was wonder how could a bank be open in a small town at this hour on a weeknight while almost all of the restaurants on the main street of a nearby larger town were firmly closed shortly after *Le Tour de France* had rolled past their doorsteps.

Back at the campground my wife prepared a wonderful dinner in the van of sautéed pork loin with mushrooms in cream sauce, once again making use of the abundant and fresh local produce. Accompanied by local white wine and finished with a few sips of Calvados, it was the perfect warm ending to a long cold day.

What is the Tour de France and why all the fuss?

The cycling race now known as *Le Tour de France* started in 1903 when the motoring newspaper *L'Auto* launched the event as a means to create publicity and boost circulation. The route of the first Tour followed the perimeter of the country and included riding at night – a practice that was stopped two years later after riders cheated while the judges could not see them in the dark.

Le Tour has taken place every year since then except for during the two world wars. For the 101st edition in 2014 the Tour consisted of 21 point-to-point rides known as "stages" for a total distance travelled of 3,700km (2,300 miles). Each stage covered between 125km and 240km (90-150 miles) and took between 3 and 4 hours.

The route of each of the stages changes every year, but the final stage always ends in Paris and the common theme is that over the course of the Tour the riders will have faced a number of climbs and descents on mountain roads as well as some stages that are fairly flat. The locations of the stages are chosen such that the riders will visit a number of different regions of the country during the course of *Le Tour*, which also allows the nation to showcase the beauty and diversity of its landscape and scenery.

The time taken by each rider to complete each stage is recorded, and the winner of the General Classification of the Tour is the rider who has completed the entire series of stages with the lowest cumulative time. Daily prizes are also awarded for the winner of each stage. Given the variety of terrain that riders must traverse throughout the three week period of the Tour, the event is an enormous test of athleticism and endurance.

To put things into perspective, the riders travel almost the distance from New York to Phoenix (or Sydney to Perth) over the space of 21 days interspersed with only two rest days. If that is not the measure of an athlete, I don't know what is!

CHAPTER SEVEN

KINGS AND PRESIDENTS

After three nights at the damp and rainy campground in Houplines, I awoke on the final morning and found the King of the Mountains in bed next to me – or so it seemed. My wife had provided a buffet for the local mosquitoes over the past three nights and had thereby earned herself the right to be covered in red polka dots, just as the Frenchman Cyril LeMoine had earned himself the right to wear the red polka dot jersey signifying him as the most proficient hill climber after Stage 5 of *Le Tour*.

While I'm sure that Monsieur LeMoine is a nice enough young man, I was glad to discover that my initial impression was mistaken. As can be imagined, my wife was none too happy about this change in her appearance and we both longed to relocate to warmer and drier climes.

Our wishes were to be answered because Stage 6 would take us in a southerly direction. The route of *Le Tour* is planned to travel in a clockwise direction around France in even-numbered years and to travel anti-clockwise in odd-numbered years. Fortunately our visit coincided with an even-numbered year which meant that the next few days would take us closer and closer to the warmth of the south-east of the country.

The ultimate success or failure of our plans to follow *Le Tour* around France depended heavily on our ability to not only navigate the roads and highways from one end of the country to the other, but also to find our way safely to the ten different campgrounds that we had booked for our accommodation.

We had rented a GPS navigation unit for this purpose, and each evening before bed we would consult our *Tour de France Programme Officiel* to decide the best location in which to park the next day to watch the race. The chosen village or hill would be entered into "Geraldine the GPS" as we called her, and we could then retire contentedly assured that Geraldine would know how to get us where we needed to go the next morning.

One of the advantages of planning our next day's route the night before was that Geraldine would tell us not only how far we were planning to drive, but also how long it would take to get to our chosen destination. This in turn allowed us to set our alarm accordingly to allow time for the unpredictable adventure of the morning shower excursion and a quick cup of coffee before we pulled up stakes and headed out for the day.

On the morning that I woke up next to Cyril LeMoine we had set our alarm for 5.30am, or so we thought. In fact the alarm had been set for 5.30pm which would have provided us with a most luxurious sleep-in except for the fact that I awoke for some reason at 6am. I'm not sure why – perhaps it was the red dots glowing in the dark next to me that penetrated my closed eyelids.

Even though we left the campground 30 minutes later than we expected, we were not concerned because we knew Geraldine would guide us safely on our two-hour drive to Roucy in the Picardy region where we would watch the race, and then two hours further on to our next campground at Jaulny in the Lorraine region. This all meant that after the first two stages in northern France we were now finally heading in a direction under Geraldine's reliable guidance that would bring us four hours closer to the sun. It was now becoming our custom to pick up a pair of fresh-baked croissants each morning after we left the campground in order to fortify ourselves for the arduous task ahead of finding a place to park on the race route, followed by making breakfast in the van, often followed in turn by a nap or the leisurely reading of the local newspaper.

Fortunately almost every small town seemed to have a choice of at least two artisanal bakeries offering a tempting array of breads, baguettes and pastries so we seldom had to deny ourselves for more than 15 minutes before pulling the van to the side of the road to park temporarily among the local customers who were buying supplies to last them through the morning. Most bakeries in fact would close for a few hours after lunch, only to reopen later in the afternoon with a fresh array of temptations more suited to the evening meal.

Perhaps it was the fact that we had shared a deliciously flaky, sweet and raisin-studded *viennoise* pastry that morning in addition to our usual croissant, or that our hasty departure due to our misinformed alarm clock had caused us to skip our morning cup of coffee, but after two hours of driving along the *autoroute* (freeway) through lush green rolling countryside we were apparently not quite as alert as we ought to have been.

Following Geraldine's instructions, we exited the *autoroute* and drove through the town of Berry-au-Bac whose roads and boulevards had been decorated with a multitude of floral arrangements in celebration of *Le Tour*. We then continued to drive through some picturesque and vineyard-studded Picardy countryside for about 15 minutes until Geraldine guided us back to the *autoroute*.

At this point a rational person might have asked himself why the GPS system would have guided him through this unexpected but highly enjoyable detour from the *autoroute*. But on the other hand, what rational person would get out of bed on vacation at 6am and drive hundreds of miles for the purpose of watching a bunch of grown men riding past on their bikes? And do it almost every day for 3 weeks?

Quite accordingly therefore, we continued merrily on our way on the *autoroute* for another 20 minutes until it slowly dawned on us that we had not only missed finding our intended viewing location of Roucy, but had also passed Reims which was where the finish of the day's stage would take place, and were now heading away from Reims and on towards the campground in Jaulny. Of course by the time we realized what had happened we had passed a number of exits from the *autoroute* and had to drive another 30 minutes before we could find a place to turn around. To add insult to injury we managed to take a wrong turn after we had turned around, costing ourselves another 20 minutes or so.

It's at times like these that I am yet again reminded of the folk wisdom of my grandmother who used to say "Don't feel sorry for yourself. There is always someone worse off than you." As things turned out that "someone" was soon to be found right in front of me.

Allow me to explain. Unlike the interstate highway systems in the US and Australia which is funded by governments and taxes, the *autoroute* system in France relies heavily on tolls. On almost every day of our journey around France we encountered a number of toll plazas – some of which even accepted credit cards on occasion, but don't get me started again on that subject. Our unplanned rerouting on this particular day caused us to encounter quite a few more toll plazas than normal, and it was at one of these highway robbery locations that we saw that particular "someone" who was worse off than we were.

The car in front of us was from Great Britain according its registration plate, and indeed the steering wheel was on the right side of the cabin as is the case in many countries outside mainland Europe. We had seen numerous British cars and camper vans up until this point and had given them little thought among the vehicles we had seen from other countries.

The man driving this British car was alone in his vehicle and in order to pay the toll at the machine on the left side of the traffic lane, he was obliged to open his door, exit the vehicle and then walk around the car to access the toll machine. Thinking of how many toll plazas we had already encountered and how many more were yet to come made us forget our troubles and be grateful that we weren't in the shoes of this poor Brit who had to not only get out of his car at every single toll booth but also risk the ire of those other drivers waiting impatiently behind him.

I'm sure he must have wished he had brought a friend along with him to France to sit in the passenger seat and negotiate with the toll machines. I wanted to tell him where he could find someone who would be available to work for hire, but alas he had left before I had a chance to give him directions to the bistro near the camper van depot outside Paris.

After this series of misadventures we finally arrived at Roucy at 11.45am – just 15 minutes before the roads would be closed for the race. Somehow we had managed to turn a two-hour journey into almost 5 hours of sightseeing, detours and toll plazas. We had encountered a number of reminders of World War 2 along the way in the form of cemeteries and monuments of different kinds. Indeed the wide and flower-decorated main street of one of the villages we drove through was named Franklin Roosevelt Boulevard.

We parked Gisèle just outside the entrance to Roucy, at a crossroads with open grassy space on all sides that had attracted a number of camper vans. As is the case in most of the towns that *Le Tour* passes through, the local residents had decorated the intersection and its surrounds with flowers and signs welcoming the traveling circus that is *Le Tour de France*. At one of the corners of the intersection a busload of children about 6-7 years old was impatiently waiting for the first signs of the Publicity Caravan while their guardians tried to keep them entertained with games and other physical activities.

It had rained on and off throughout the morning and no doubt the children and their caretakers were hoping that the sun would make an appearance and chase away the grey skies. Just as we were thinking the same thing there appeared a man who brought the sunshine with him.

Heaven only knows what possesses a balding man in his 40s who decides to dress as a giant bee while watching the world's greatest bicycle race, but apparently the same spirit possesses him every year at the same time. Psychiatrists may debate among themselves the meaning of the giant fly swatter that the King Bee carries with him, but there is no debating the fact that he enjoys himself.

Shortly after his arrival he decided to walk over towards the group of children and offer some entertainment. Just before he reached the waiting youngsters he tried to make friends with a small dog on a leash. The dog was having none of this and barked and backed away as the Bee tried to lean down to pat him. Happily he received a warmer welcome from the children and he soon had them singing songs and playing games. The adults escorting the children must have thanked their lucky stars for the arrival of the Bee, as would anyone who has ever tried to keep a group of energetic youngsters entertained on a rainy day.

While we awaited the arrival of the Caravan, I braved the windy and cold elements to hang two banners on our van advertising the blog that I was writing each day called "It's Only A Bike Race". I would hang these banners each day after we parked: one on the side of the van facing the roadway and the other on the roof. In yet another example of outsmarting myself, while sitting safely in my Texas living room I had imagined that a banner on the roof of the van could not help but be seen by the helicopters flying overhead and broadcasting the race to the world. However as I found out, in reality the helicopters do not fly low enough to allow the lettering on a roof banner to be clearly seen. Nevertheless I continued to put the banner on the roof each day for the first half of *Le Tour* before later giving up and moving it to a location on the van where it would be seen by the oncoming cars and riders.

Given the conditions on this day it was difficult to get the banner up on to the roof without it being caught by the wind and blown off. After watching me fail with several attempts to get the banner in place, a local lady who had been waiting in a nearby car asked if I wanted help. I threw a rope over to her, the banner was quickly put in place and I thanked her for her kindness. This was yet another spontaneous gesture of kindness among the many we had already witnessed and benefitted from during our journey in France. We had also noted that drivers on roads and *autoroutes* very often make space to allow other cars into their lane or wave others to go ahead of them in heavy, slow-moving traffic situations.

After the banners were safely installed I bought the latest edition of the daily sporting newspaper *L'Équipe* from a passing truck that preceded the Caravan. The first seven pages were dedicated to comprehensive – if rather breathless – coverage of *Le Tour*. The entire front page was taken up by a photograph of the current race leader Vincenzo Nibali during the previous day's stage. The close-up photo showed Nibali covered in spattered mud from the cobblestones and the all-caps headline read "DANTESQUE". The subheading read "The inferno of the Nord region kept its promises". It seemed to me to be somewhat of a literary stretch to compare the cold and rainy conditions of the previous day to Dante's Inferno, but I had to agree it must have been a hellish day for the riders. In complete contrast, the entire back page of the paper was devoted to NASCAR and a profile of Dale Earnhart Jr.

More spectators arrived on foot as the scheduled time for the arrival of the Caravan drew closer. Others arrived in cars, only to encounter the gendarmes who would wag a metronomic index finger at those who arrived with ambitions of passing in directions that were *barrée* (closed). Meanwhile the busload of children continued to look longingly up the road in anticipation.

Finally the Caravan arrived and provided great excitement for spectators of all ages, throwing out hats, tote bags, key rings, detergent samples, snacks, inflatable pillows and numerous other small giveaway items to the eager spectators. The crowd was in good spirits, and the smiles on faces were not diminished when the Vittel truck sprayed them with misted water on this cold day. Many of the families with young children - contented with their haul of trinkets and samples - left after the Caravan had passed rather than wait another hour or more for the riders to arrive.

About 20 minutes before the riders were due to arrive in Roucy, two black helicopters with *Tour de France* logos painted on their sides landed in a field opposite us. The landing site was just behind the children who were glued to the whole event with little noses strained against a wire-mesh fence. The big news was that Francois Hollande, the President of the Republic of France, was at today's stage.

Just before the helicopter landing it had been broadcast on the web that *Monsieur* Hollande was riding in the car of the Tour Director, Christian Prudhomme. The logic of providing security for important people would say that it does not make sense that the vehicle in which the President was traveling would be identified so clearly and publicly, however the arrival of the helicopters would explain the very unusual and heavy presence of gendarmes at our location.

Perhaps the earlier announcement was a diversion and the President was in fact in a helicopter instead of a car. The fact that both helicopters departed immediately after the riders had passed through the town tends to support this position. I must admit that I'm still trying not to be offended by being ignored like this. I left the following message on his voicemail (at least I think it was *Monsieur* Hollande's number that the operator gave me when I called for information): "So Francois, I heard you were in town – and you didn't call?"

Meanwhile the mystery of the occupants of the two helicopters is something that I remain unable to answer - at least until Francois returns my call.

The first of the riders to arrive was a group of four who had broken away from the peleton and had established a lead of 50 seconds when they passed us. All four athletes looked comfortable with 59 kilometers remaining in the stage, but they were about to be tested by two steep hills on the other side of Roucy. As so often happens, the last of the breakaway riders was eventually caught and passed by the peleton with 13 kilometers remaining in the stage. The best result on the day from any of the breakaway four was from the Spanish rider Luis Angel Mate Mardones who finished in 144th position, 4 minutes and 13 seconds behind the winner of the stage.

This pattern of a breakaway rider or group being caught by the peleton is repeated constantly throughout each stage of the race. Due to the slipstream effect, it is estimated that a person who rides behind another rider saves up to 25-30% of his energy. In some cases, right in the middle of the peleton it is estimated that riders can save up to 50% of their energy. This all means that the riders who have conserved their energy in the bunch behind the breakaway group have a good chance of being able to overtake the breakaway riders – as long as they do not leave it too late to make their move. Sometimes the peleton simply misjudges the ability of the breakaway group to hold its lead, and on other occasions the breakaway group prevails because none of the teams in the peleton is willing to lead the chase to catch it.

After the riders had passed by, my wife and I had a brief conversation with a lady about her large hairy dog that we had been admiring. She told us that he was 1 year old and a hunting dog. She then asked if we had a dog. I told her about our similarly large hairy dog and then I asked if she lived nearby. She replied:

"Oui, juste au coin"

(Yes, just around the corner)

This term is the French equivalent of a 'country mile" which means the lady might live anywhere from 100 meters to 10 kilometers away. Even though my wife does not speak French, I translated for her and the three of us were able to share the universal connection of pet lovers.

After the riders and team cars had all passed, we walked partway into the town while waiting for the traffic to disperse. This allowed us to see what an enormous event the *Tour de France* had been for Roucy, with many residents decorating their houses and hosting family and friends at outdoor tables along the route. Home-made race jerseys of all types hung on fences, balconies and flagpoles along with handwritten signs exhorting favorite riders.

On returning to Gisèle we found that the gendarmes had done a fabulous job of directing traffic after the event and the crossroads where we had parked was almost empty. We stopped at a supermarket on the way back to the *autoroute* to resume our journey towards Jaulny, and found ourselves parked next to the camper van belonging to the Bee. Once inside the supermarket we noted that the man in question had changed back into civilian clothes, however he was accompanied by his son of about 9 years in age who was dressed in a bee costume. It's good to know the family business has a future.

As we headed south on our way to Jaulny we saw the sun for the first time in a few days and passed several large fields

of sunflowers. It was reassuring to think that we were on our way to a warmer environment where we might even see some real bees.

How come that guy is wearing a yellow jersey?

Le Tour de France awards prizes in several different categories apart from that for the man who finishes with the lowest time at the end of the three weeks. Not all riders are good at riding up mountains, nor is everyone good at riding fast for short distances (sprinting), and even fewer riders at good at both. For this reason the organizers of the Tour award prizes for the best mountain climber and best sprinter each day and for the entire Tour overall.

Riders accumulate points in these categories on each stage and the highest score in each category at the finish of the Tour wins the honor of "King of the Mountains" or "Points Classification". At the end of the first stage of the Tour the winner of that stage is awarded a yellow jersey, or *maillot jaune*, which identifies him as the leader in the General Classification. In the same way, the rider who scores the most climbing points on the first stage is awarded a white jersey with red polka-dots and the rider who has scored the most sprinting points is awarded a green jersey. These riders wear their special jerseys for the next day's stage and are able to continue to wear that jersey through subsequent stages until another rider has beaten their time or point score.

All of this means that at the end of each day's stage, prizes are awarded to that day's winners in each category and then the overall leaders in each category are announced at which point one or more of the special jerseys may change hands. There is also another category for the best rider under 25 years of age, and this honor is signified by a white jersey.

CHAPTER EIGHT

CALLING ALL CANADIANS

The first thing I saw through the window on the morning, after spending the night at our new campground at Jaulny was two wild rabbits, peacefully grazing on the grass covering an unoccupied campsite. I initially wondered if they were part of the landscaping staff, constantly mowing the lawns and keeping the weeds down, but it's more likely that their most valued contribution to the wellbeing of the campground and its visitors will eventually be in the form of an addition to the restaurant menu.

Geraldine had successfully navigated us to the campground the night before, and we found it to be located in a mountainous setting that called for us to cross a single-lane wooden bridge over a ravine. The campground itself was quite tranquil, consisting mostly of open green space interrupted only by the occasional camper van or tent. As we drove to our appointed space we encountered a young couple holding hands as they walked across to their tent which was pitched on the edge of another ravine, well away from any other campers. It seemed that they wanted to be alone – perhaps so they could read *L'Équipe* without interruption or plot a route to their next destination that would allow them to avoid all toll roads. In any case it looked like they had a found themselves a nice quiet place to pursue whatever activities they may have had in mind. I imagined there must be a beautiful view from their vantage point, perhaps a clear mountain stream running below them and a view across the ravine to the mountains beyond. However I did not walk over to see for myself for fear of breaking the concentration of the young couple in their tranquil solitude.

When morning came I discovered that this particular campground offered the most generous ration of shower water that we had so far encountered, with a decadent, nay sinful 45 seconds per burst. As if this cornucopia of luxury were not enough, I also discovered that if I pressed the shower button again before the 45 seconds had expired the timer would reset and provide me with another 45 seconds of heaven. By judicious use of this feature one could achieve a continuous stream of water just like a real shower.

And I was not alone in my bliss. My wife also made the discovery that she had been using the "cool" setting on her hair dryer ever since she bought it a few days earlier. While she had noted that the dryer was not as warm as those she used at home, she had explained to herself that it must be that hair dryers in France are made without a hot setting because French women don't want to risk damaging their hair. Having now discovered the "hot" setting, my wife was able to dry her hair in her normal manner in half the time it had previously taken.

The morning light had also brought with it one more important discovery, albeit probably not quite as pleasant for those involved. We had heard the distant sounds of trains throughout the night, with the comforting rumbling sound and occasional horn blast carrying across the night air. Another train came into earshot while I was walking back from the shower and it was then that I realized that the ravine overlooking which the romantic young couple had pitched their tent contained not a bucolic mountain stream as I had thought, but a busy and very active main railway line that had been obscured from view by trees. I would imagine that between one thing and another the couple had experienced a very restless night.

As we left the campground on our way to go watch Stage 7, Geraldine contrived to navigate us on to a single-lane dirt road on the side of a steep hill. After about 400 meters she decided that she had made a mistake and advised us to "turn around when possible". However turning around was not possible and after wondering whether Geraldine was still mad at us for ignoring her original directions to guide us to Roucy the day before, we retraced our tracks for 400 meters in reverse gear.

Stage 7 was to finish in the city of Nancy in the region of Lorraine. While the city has a rich history dating back to the earliest known settlement there in 800 BC, I could not help but think about its name and the possible consequences it may give rise to in the 21st century AD.

Imagine this scene for me if you will. A lovely young French lady living in the Lorraine region is visiting her mother in Paris to tell her the good news of her forthcoming engagement to a local young man. *Maman* is of course overjoyed with the news until she asks her daughter more about her fiancé and then breaks into tears.

Daughter: "What's the matter *maman*? All I said is that he's a Nancy boy."

Mother: *(Between sobs)* Yes, I heard you! Now I'll *never* have grandchildren! *(Sobs uncontrollably)*

This was to be our first opportunity to observe *Le Tour* in a location that included mountains. We parked Gisèle 17 kilometers from the finish line on a long uphill stretch of road that the papers predicted would separate the riders from one another as they tackled the challenging climb. This would allow us to observe the individual competitors more closely as they would likely be in a long series of single file groups when they passed us. This would be a welcome contrast to some of the other days when the riders swooped by us in a short-lived frenzy of color.

While waiting for the action to begin we walked down the hill into the little town of Maron which had clearly been anticipating the arrival of this day for some months. Along the way we met two Englishmen next to a large Union Jack waving in the breeze. My first thought was to congratulate them on their wise decision to travel together and thereby speed up the process of dealing with the toll booths. Instead we commiserated with them about the unfortunate withdrawal of their compatriot Chris Froome and they explained that this is why they were in the process of redoing their roadside signs in favor of Richie Porte, the Sky team's number two rider. Then one of them added with a resigned air "We came to the Tour to support Froome and now we find ourselves cheering for a bloody Tasmanian." Leaving them to contemplate the unfortunate turn of events that had caused two self-respecting English gents to turn their allegiance towards a Tasmanian, we walked on.

Further down the hill after the wall-to-wall line of camper vans had ended we met two Canadians standing alone together on the side of the road under a large Canadian flag. We soon saw that one of them was in the process of getting dressed in a full Canadian Mountie uniform. They were both 60ish in age and the Mountie explained  that he figures that if he places himself far enough away from the crowds of people, he will have less competition when it comes to meeting the women who will be undoubtedly be attracted by his uniform. While I was still pondering his logic and thinking that such women would have to go well out of their way to find him when he's standing on an empty stretch of road, I turned and found the other Canadian had donned a large poncho made in the design of the Canadian flag. Making a mental note to keep an eye out for any women who looked as if they might be searching the hills and mountains of the Vosges region for a Canadian mounted policeman, we walked on and soon reached the edge of the village.

All along the route through Maron residents were hosting lunch gatherings on their front verandah, front lawn, front balcony and even on the footpath in front of the house. The accompanying decorations and flags that had been placed on houses, poles, fences and buildings served to create a very festive atmosphere.

It was not surprising that the local residents were in such a celebratory mood. I had read in the paper that it had been 10

years since *Le Tour* was in this part of the country. We encountered several cafés on the main street with tables set outside, populated by middle-aged men who looked like they were prepared for a long stay if one were to judge by the ample provisions at hand on the table. They were clearly determined not to die of thirst while waiting for the *Le Tour*.

We passed one house hosting a gathering on their upstairs balcony and displaying a sign that translated to "Thank you for bringing the Tour de France past my house on my 11th birthday. Leane."

As we walked past the house we looked up to find a girl of about that age sitting at one end of the row of chairs with around 10 adults. I called up to her

"Bonne fête, Leane!"

(Happy birthday, Leane!)

The adults all sighed collectively "Aah" and looked at her and back to us. Many of them called back to us *"Merci"* (Thank you). They seemed genuinely touched by that simple gesture on our part. Who said French people were not like the rest of us?

When the Publicity Caravan passed by we were treated to the sight of the King Bee sitting on the Skoda Super Fan float in the throne-like chair. Evidently his appearances in earlier stages of the race had created some buzz and led to him being honored by one of the tour sponsors. There was no sign of his son, so we could only assume that the fly swatter scepter had been passed temporarily to the young fellow at the side of the road where he would do his part to uphold the family tradition.

When the riders arrived they were indeed spread out, as we had hoped. They passed within 3 feet of us and we made eye contact with several of them – no doubt they noticed the contented look on our faces after my uninterrupted shower and my wife's thermally-enhanced hairstyle. My wife and I both had to agree that the experience of seeing *Le Tour* in person is infinitely better than watching it on television, although somewhat harder to arrange.

After the riders and cars had passed we drove down into the village and found large numbers of people clustered around the entrance to several doorways along the main street. After a moment we realized they were trying to catch the closing parts of the stage in nearby Nancy on television. We wondered if there were any Nancy boys among the crowd and kept our distance just in case.

Once again the gendarmes did an excellent job of clearing out the traffic after the race and we were soon on our way to our next campground, near Sanchey. With Geraldine's help we arrived at Sanchey but could not find the campground at *Lac de Bouzey* (in English this would be pronounced Boozy Lake).

After circling fruitlessly around a couple of times we finally stopped and asked a man on the street for directions, showing him a printout of the name and address we were searching for. He turned around 180 degrees and with good humor pointed to the sign and entrance to the campground.

We were directly across the street from it. No wonder Geraldine gets mad at us.

After getting settled in we ordered a dinner of *moules et frites* (mussels and French fries) at a local restaurant overlooking the lake. The service was a bit slow to begin with and we reminded ourselves that the custom in France is to take food seriously and not just rush in, throw some food down and rush out again. After struggling to finish the large pot of mussels, the waitress wanted to know if we would like more – apparently the 19 Euro (US $25) price per person included an endless supply of mussels. We declined but the English couple at the table next to us accepted the offer with relish.

The waitress then offered us a dessert of strawberries Melba. This turned out to be large parfait glass with fresh strawberries buried under a mound of tasty whipped cream. We both felt thoroughly spoiled as well as thoroughly full after finishing our dinner in such style.

Before our meal arrived, a bus load of about 15 middle-aged ladies had arrived and were guided to a long table near us. After much fussing around about who would sit where, eventually they all got seated and continued to talk happily among themselves. We wondered if they were a school reunion group because they all seemed to be about the same age.

While we were eating, a French guitarist started playing on the other side of the dining area singing British and American songs including Hotel California and Sweet Home Alabama. After a while he invited the restaurant patrons to sing along with the chorus of some of his songs, most notably Hey Jude which was raucously celebrated by all concerned.

By now the ladies were all in good form and one of them got up on her chair for a few moments. A few minutes later when the guitarist played Hound Dog, two of the other ladies got up and danced a spirited jive next to their table as we and the other diners clapped along. Later after our dessert when we got up to leave, we went to say good bye to the ladies' table.

They all seem disappointed that we were going, especially the dance-on-chair lady. When I described our planned trip around France she said to me "I want to go with you". There was much laughter all around as I gave her my card with the blog address and told her she could go with me on the web.

Who said French people aren't friendly, and where were those Canadian guys when I needed them?

Why do they have teams if only one guy can win in each category?

There are 22 teams in the 2014 Tour de France, each of which has 9 riders. The ultimate aim for each team is to have its leader win the General Classification. Millions of dollars in prize money and sponsorship are attached to the prestige of being the rider who finishes the last day of the Tour with the yellow jersey.

The teams also are awarded points on each stage of the Tour and although there are no special jerseys involved, there are daily and overall prizes awarded to the leading team. Because of the extremely challenging physical requirements placed on a rider who would aim to win the final yellow jersey, riders with such capabilities are few and far between. For that reason many teams set their sights on the other prize categories while they try to build a team capable of winning higher honors. No matter what its particular goal may be, the members of a team need to work together towards that goal. For example if a team is trying to win the yellow jersey, the individual team members must be prepared to sacrifice their own ambitions for the sake of the team leader. They do this by riding close to their leader, often taking it in turns to ride in front of him to set the pace and allow him to conserve energy by riding in their slipstream.

Another example of teamwork is often seen in the closing parts of a mountain stage where the leader may be at or near the front of the field and a rival from another team tries to break away from the group and gain time on the leader. In this case one of the leader's teammates who is a climbing specialist will stand up on his bike and chase down the breakaway while the leader follows and eventually catches up. In both these examples the teammates will often have exhausted themselves before the finish line, but they have done their job in supporting their leader.

It is for these reasons that every winner of the overall yellow jersey at the finish line in Paris makes sure to publicly thank his teammates and share his winnings with them because he knows he could not have done it alone.

CHAPTER NINE

THE TALE OF THE TAPE

The day began with the most pleasant surprise that the showers at "Boozy Lake" were the hottest we had encountered since our arrival in France one week earlier. This combined with my newly-discovered trick of pressing the shower button in such a way as to ensure a continuous flow of water seemed to diminish the impact of the grey skies and rain that we had experienced each day up to this point.

Not only was this campground equipped with an efficient hot water supply, it also had a small convenience store on site that sold fresh bread and pastries. Thus the daily quest to find a bakery somewhere along the route to the race was resolved even before we left the campground. All of this was wonderful news because this campground was to be our home base for the next four days. It's funny how small things such as a hot shower and flaky croissant to start the day can make such a difference to one's outlook on life.

Perhaps inspired by our new surroundings, my wife volunteered to take on the role of driving Gisèle to our race viewing point for the day. With the trusty assistance of Geraldine, she took us to the town of Vagney in the Vosges

Mountains. This town is located at the foot of the first of three climbs that were scheduled to take place during the final 30 kilometers of Stage 8.

Having seen first-hand the previous day the improved spectator experience that comes from watching an uphill stretch, we parked Gisèle about 25 kilometers from the finish, part way up the climb leading to the peak known as the *Col de la Croix des Moinats*. Once again learning from experience, we parked with the van facing downhill. This would allow us not only to sit in comfort while we watched the road waiting for signs of the Caravan or Tour riders, but also to use the windscreen wipers as necessary to clear our view.

Having thus arranged our viewing location we looked around and found that we had parked outside a house that was being built below the road level and which had a spectacular view of the valley behind it. Not long after we arrived, a grumpy couple with two children aged about 10 and 12 arrived at the house to do some work on the property. It appeared that they were the owners of the house and it seemed that they were entirely untouched by the festive spirit of *Le Tour de France* that seemed to have affected residents in all of the other towns and villages that we had so far visited. All four members of the family looked decidedly unhappy about the intrusion of *Le Tour* on their little piece of paradise.

The entrance to the driveway had already been barred with plastic tape prior to our arrival but just in case anyone had missed the point, *Monsieur* emerged dramatically shortly after his arrival and used iron stakes and tape to seal off the entire frontage of the house while his wife and family looked on defiantly. I found it somewhat difficult to follow his train of thought, because anyone trying to drive on to the property outside of the driveway would need to negotiate a steep and muddy drop several meters down an embankment before likely becoming stuck in the mud outside the front door of the house.

Nevertheless in his own mind *Monsieur* had made a bold statement to the world that not even the slightest hint of trespassing would be tolerated on his property. I watched to see whether he would next obtain some longer poles to use to tape off the roof of the house to warn the television helicopters not to intrude on his sacred property.

However the family packed up and left after about an hour, carefully closing the tape over the driveway behind them. Sadly for me this meant that they were not present a couple of hours later before the Caravan arrived to see a *Tour de France* official remove and discard all of the carefully-placed stakes and tape. It would have been intriguing to watch the undoubtedly excited discussion between all parties.

After the homeowner entertainment had ended we walked down into the village. As had been the case in other towns we saw people hosting lunches along the route in their front yards and any other available locations with a view of the road. But compared to other towns that we had seen, the street and house decorations were quite sparse – perhaps due to the heavy rain that was forecast for later in the day.

We passed a number of families on our walk, some with small babies, all waiting for the Publicity Caravan to arrive with all of its color, noise and of course giveaways. It was remarkable how patient the children seemed to be while they waited, as they amused themselves with card games or other small diversions that did not involve pecking away on a cell phone or pestering their parents.

On the side of the road at the foot of the hill, a parked van with an Australian flag hanging over the driver's window caught my eye. The van was labelled "Australians On Tour Cycling", but there was no-one inside. We had earlier seen an older couple wearing New Zealand shirts riding their bikes up the hill. I tried to engage them with a greeting but there was no response or flicker of recognition whatsoever – my guess is that all of their available oxygenated blood supply was being used by their legs, with no reserves left over for the functioning of superfluous organs such as their ears.

On the other hand, they may have been non-English-speaking Germans who had received their NZ shirts as part of the package when they bought tickets for the Lord of the Rings movie. But then again they may have been part of the cycling group associated with the Aussie-decorated van.

But there's one thing I do know for sure: if I were paying to have someone drive me to *Le Tour* so that I could ride part of a stage, I would make sure they parked the van such that my starting point was at the top of the hill and not at the bottom.

Before we left for our walk, a car with an older couple inside had pulled up and parked behind us. (I can only wonder what they might have done if not for the strong deterrent factor of the tape across the front of the property.) Not long after returning from our walk, my wife noticed out of the corner of her eye something happening in the space between Gisèle and the other car. She turned just in time to see *Madame* from the car behind us - who was of ample proportions and cast a large shadow even on a gloomy day - pulling up a large pair of floral bloomers after relieving herself on the grass. I was grateful to have missed the spectacle and hoped for her sake there was no poison ivy in the immediate vicinity.

Rain showers came and went while we waited for the Caravan, and more families arrived apparently unperturbed by the inclement weather. Luckily the rain held off for the duration of the passing of the Caravan and the children who had waited so patiently were well rewarded for their efforts. Alas the Carrefour tablecloth so desired by my wife continued to elude her, even as our stockpile of goodies from other companies represented in the Caravan continued to grow.

The rain recommenced in force after the Caravan had finished parading by, and many families decided to go home and count their spoils rather than wait for the cyclists. Several other families, obviously made of sterner stuff, retreated under trees to wait out the next hour before the cyclists were due to appear.

A breakaway of five riders eventually came into view - including Simon Yates from Orica-GreenEdge - as they climbed the hillside road leading past our position. This group was more than 7 minutes ahead of the peleton with 25 kilometers left to the finish line, but most of this remaining distance was uphill which would present a challenge to the breakaway riders as they tried to maintain their lead. The riders in the peleton would have to face the same climbs, but their legs would be relatively less tired than those of the breakaway group.

The breakaway group had started to split up by the time they passed us, and the peleton had also been broken up into a series of smaller groups. There had been much speculation about the favored Spanish rider Alberto Contador whose strength is in climbing. He began the day some two-and-a-half minutes behind the leader Vincenzo Nibali and was expected to try to catch up some time in today's mountains in order to diminish the gap between the two. Both riders were in the midst of the main bunch when they passed us, with no sign of any attempt by Contador to improve his position.

By the time they reached the finish line 25 kilometers and three steep climbs later, Contador had worked hard and finished second in the stage, gaining a few seconds on Nibali in the process and improving his overall race standing from 16th place to 6th. Simon Yates who had shared the lead for most of the day ended up in 43rd place in the stage after riding 100 miles in a fraction less than four hours. I figured he and all of his fellow competitors would have no trouble falling asleep later that night.

But as challenging as the day's route was for the riders, the next two stages would be more mountainous and thus even more difficult for the riders. I'm pretty sure that by the time we get to the French Alps there will be a number of riders who would have come to the realization that my method of touring the beautiful countryside of France is far superior to theirs. I just hope we can make room in Gisèle for a few extra passengers. We'll keep an eye out for hitch-hikers wearing lycra shorts.

A Week in the Life of a Camper Van

Bonjour et excusez-moi for the intrusion! My name is Gisèle and I am an elegant camper van based on the chassis of a 21-foot Fiat Ducato truck. I know I am only young, just 8,054 kilometers old, but I have to tell you that this past week I have carried two passengers like I have never carried before. They speak a strange language (especially the man) and they have habits that can only be described as odd. Allow me to explain, if you will.

The man has the most curious habit of head-butting every possible overhead shelf and cupboard at least two or three times each day. At first I thought it was accidental but he does it so often I have come to realize that he must be doing it for some strange reason only known to him. Perhaps he is trying to see whether his wooden head is harder than my wooden cupboards, but I know for certain that my cupboards and shelves are solid wood and they do not make a hollow sound like his head does when hit.

And you cannot imagine the way the woman handles my highly technical 6-speed manual gear shift. Evidently she cannot count from 1 to 6 without counting the same number twice, or going backwards, or starting from 3 instead of 1. *Sacré bleu!*

Even though I have a luxurious shower room only slightly smaller than an old-style telephone booth and equipped with a shower curtain that is guaranteed to cling when wet to anyone who takes a shower, for some reason they have decided instead to use the shower facilities at the campgrounds every morning.

I have served them well in spite of all this daily mistreatment and lack of appreciation, taking them to *Le Tour de France* every day without complaint. And after I have safely parked at the side of the road, among others of my kind (although they are not as beautiful or elegant as I am) these tasteless cretins insist on hanging vulgar advertising signs on me – even on my roof - and covering my attractive paintwork. And the orange-and-white signs do not even match my tasteful color palette!

Although they are not aware of it, every day I have my revenge for this uncaring cruelty. One of my two lovely skylights is located right above their bed, and the other above my spacious kitchen/dining room. It so happened that it rained during the first night they spent with me, and they were so busy banging their heads and trying to connect the electric cable that they did not close the skylights when they retired. Of course I did not alert them to this oversight and needless to say, when they awoke in the morning their ardor had been – shall we say – dampened.

Even better, they are awakened early every single morning by the light shining directly on them through the skylight over their bed. They do not know it, but there is an internal nightshade that can be drawn over the skylight to help them get a full night's sleep. There is no sign or symbol to indicate that such a shade exists, so I will simply let them find out for themselves.

But my favorite trick – my *pièce de résistance* - is to randomly fling open a drawer or cupboard door while they are driving, making the non-driver risk life and limb to go back and close the offending aperture while I twist and turn around the winding roads.

Only two more weeks to go before I return to a more civilized life with more civilized passengers. But I am quite sure that *Monsieur*'s hollow wooden head will crack open long before then.

CHAPTER TEN

PARKING AMIDST THE PLAGUE

Up until this point of our trip, we had observed each day's action in *Le Tour* by selecting a general vicinity somewhere along the route and then parking on the side of the road and enjoying the comforts offered by Gisèle while we waited for the Publicity Caravan to pass by followed by the riders and their support vehicles. We had learned early on that parking on a flat stretch of road would afford us only a fleeting glimpse of the riders as they flashed past us in a blur of colors and a whirr of finely-tuned wheels, and so we had changed our tactics to park on an uphill stretch where the pace of the riders would necessarily be slower.

For Stage 9, which would start in the pretty Lorraine town of Gérardmer and end in Mulhouse in the province of Alsace, we changed our tactics again and decided to watch the start of the stage and then drive on to a vantage point further along the route to see the riders a second time.

.Gérardmer is located high in the Vosges Mountains and is home to a number of ski resorts in its immediate area. The level of interest in *Le Tour* from residents and visitors alike was very high, not only because the previous day's stage had ended in Gérardmer but also because this was only the second time that the town had ever hosted the event. My wife and I had visited this lovely town on previous visits to France but had thought it was our own little secret beauty spot. But apparently the organizers of *Le Tour*, in their wisdom, had decided it was once again time to share the beauty of Gérardmer with the rest of the world.

Thanks to the aforementioned organizers, vehicle traffic was very busy as we got close to the town center where the start of the stage would take place. Nevertheless we were still able to fleetingly capture some attractive views of the beautiful mountain lake around which the town is built.

As we drew closer to the town center we discovered what can best be described as a plague of white camper vans lining the streets. They were parked along the side of the road, in parking lots and wall-to-wall in the campground next to the lake. (We of course did not consider ourselves to be part of the plague, because Gisèle was a stylish silver-grey rather than a garish white.)

Given the number of large vehicles that were in the area, I began to grow anxious about finding a parking spot for ourselves. I did not fancy the idea of parking on the footpath, even though I knew that other adventurous souls would surely do so before the end of the day despite the risk of being towed. Mentally weighing up a quick strategy review of the whole idea of parking on the footpath, I figured it would take a large and specialized vehicle to tow a camper van and surely such vehicles would be few and far between in a town of 9,250 inhabitants. But on the other hand the fee to recover a camper van from a towing impound site would surely be high enough to attract the requisite operators from all over the country along with their enabling hardware while also imposing a significant penalty on unsuspecting visitors such as myself who would provide easy prey.

While inching along the streets looking for a parking place I mentally created the framework of a business school exercise to assess the business case for a tow truck operator to follow *Le Tour* each year as it traveled around the country, towing vehicles in one town before moving on to the next. The type of target vehicle to be towed would be one variable in the calculations along with the relative purchase cost of a towing vehicle and the amount of fuel used to follow the race around France.

But as good luck would have it, just before I encased myself totally within the paralysis of analysis, we found an available space in a parking lot located only two blocks from where the day's *Tour de France* activities would all take place.

A platform had been set up on the main street for the purpose of hosting the events together with a giant video screen nearby. A large crowd had gathered and we watched as the individual elements of the Publicity Caravan were introduced one after the other with the Carrefour organization well represented. Hats, key rings, sunshades, inflatable pillows and other goodies were thrown from the floats in the same manner that we had experienced along the roads, and the competition to gather up these prizes was fierce among the small children scurrying among the crowd like terriers chasing after a rat. And if a certain tablecloth had been thrown at random into the crowd from the passing Caravan I might well have seen a different side of my wife, but perhaps fortunately this was not to be as no tablecloths were sighted.

After the Caravan was safely on its way to Mulhouse we saw two couples carrying Australian flags and wearing matching headgear. I asked them if they were travelling in that white camper van that I happened to see on the edge of town. They replied that they have indeed rented two white camper vans, which when I thought about it made sense because I can't imagine how two middle-aged couples could live together for an extended period in one camper van without resulting in the launch of court proceedings of one kind or another.

Under such circumstances of living in close quarters for an extended period I would think that thoughts of divorce and/or strangulation would cross people's minds quite frequently. For this reason I would imagine that each individual would be well advised to have stored the telephone numbers of a matrimonial attorney and criminal defense attorney on speed dial in his or her mobile phone before departing from home.

However not only did these Australian couples have the good sense to rent separate vehicles but they also added an extra stroke of genius to relieve the stress of navigating a large vehicle around the wrong side of the winding and narrow roads of France. Killing two birds with one stone, both couples had found a way to distinguish their particular square white camper vans from all others around them by the way they turned their rear-mounted bike racks into wine racks. In one foul swoop they had managed to create an instant source of relief from the stress of both identifying their own vehicle and living in a confined space with their respective spouses, with no lawyers required.

After humbly, and no doubt inadequately, congratulating them for the inherent genius manifested in this wise adaptation on their part, we headed back to our van to await the assembling of the riders for the start of Stage 9. On the way back to our parking space we saw a small crowd clustered around the doorway of the *Hotel de la Paix*, which was where one of the teams had apparently stayed overnight. The team bus was waiting outside and the riders were emerging one by one, a few minutes apart, to get on to the bus to take them through the crowds to the start area a few blocks away. The way in which people were lined up on each side of the front door was reminiscent of scenes from Hollywood where photographers and spectators are lined up waiting for some star or another to emerge from an upscale restaurant or other event.

After consulting our program we came to realize that the crowds were waiting for the Spanish rider Alberto Contador who was expected to make some bold moves during the day's race and challenge for the lead. Contador had already won *Le Tour* twice and was reportedly in peak condition to try for a third title. After a few minutes he emerged from the hotel, thereby creating much excitement among the crowd who pressed forward eagerly. He stopped to sign a few autographs and even posed for a few selfie pictures with his fans.

I thought this was quite gracious on his part because he didn't look reluctant or stressed by the attention, nor did he look as if the scrum of supporters were feeding his ego. The crowd seemed to think the same way because when he finally stepped on to the bus after a few minutes of interaction they applauded him politely and appreciatively. Compared to some of the overpaid and overindulged sports figures in the United

States, it was refreshing to see an accomplished and extremely capable athlete behave in such a humble and unassuming manner.

After resting for a while in the van we made our way back to see the riders start the race. But along the way we saw a photographer relieving himself against the hedge next to the front fence of a local residence. He was wearing a vest that said on the back "Photo Pool". Perhaps the term "Photo Puddle" would have been more *à propos* at that particular moment.

We moved on to the start point and saw the riders assembling for the start, with each of the current jersey holders being introduced to the crowd in turn. They took their place at the front of the line and were joined by the other 180 or so riders who remained after 14 of their fellow competitors had already dropped out of the race for various reasons. Together they created a mass of color on Gèrardmer's main street, flanked by an eager crowd and elegant buildings on both sides.

Across the street from us we could see the four Australians

we had met earlier. They had found themselves an elevated position with a great view of the riders from which they were waving their flags and enjoying the spectacle. We wondered how they had spent their time in the interim period after the departure of the Publicity Caravan and then mentally kicked ourselves to think that during that interval we had gone back to relax with Gisèle instead of offering to share in a sampling of the wares in their van-mounted wine racks.

At the appointed start time for the stage, and with the crowd eagerly counting down the last ten seconds, the mass of color that was the 22 teams of riders began its slow movement along the street and past our location. It was a special sight to see the jersey holders leading the way but most gratifyingly I was able to compare my wife's complexion to the King of the Mountain's red polka dot jersey and happily determine that the worst had passed after the assaults she had endured from the unrelenting mosquito squadrons of Houplines.

After looking at the grey skies above, we had earlier in the day abandoned the idea of driving to another point along the route to view the passing riders. Given that there was no further improvement in the weather we decided to retire to a local café to watch the race on television rather than doing so on the large video screen in the main square of the town. This turned out to  be a wise decision because it rained on and off throughout the afternoon while we had a corner of a quaint 1930s-vintage dining room to ourselves. While enjoying a lunch of Quiche Lorraine and Veal with Mushrooms and Cream Sauce – not to mention some local wine – we watched the day's race undisturbed by rain or traffic problems.

Surprisingly, the favored contenders Nibali, Contador and the Australian Richie Porte remained with the main group of riders throughout the stage instead of trying to gain some time on one another. As a result, the Frenchman Tony Gallopin was able to take over the yellow jersey on the eve of the French national holiday known as Bastille Day - much to the glee of the local media. Gallopin himself was thrilled with becoming the overall race leader, which he later said he had dreamed of doing since the infamous Cobblestone Stage.

After a long and enjoyable day in Gérardmer, Geraldine the GPS navigated us safely back to our campground. That evening we enjoyed our most restful night's sleep of the journey to date, thanks largely to our newly-found discovery of a shade that can be drawn over the skylight above our bed.

CHAPTER ELEVEN

FIREWORKS IN THE MOUNTAINS

"I still feel that variable gears are only for people over forty-five. Isn't it better to triumph by the strength of your muscles than by the artifice of a derailer? We are getting soft... As for me, give me a fixed gear!"

HENRI DESGRANGE

Founder of *Le Tour de France*

Since July 14th is France's national day, it is the equivalent of July 4th in the United States or January 26th in Australia. As such I am reminded of the comment made by an American acquaintance a few years ago during the course of a discussion of national holidays: "So your July 4th is in January? How weird!"

Which in turn reminds me of a comment from an Australian colleague some years ago when I told him I was about to relocate overseas with my work: "Australia is the best country in the world. Why would you want to go anywhere else?" It should be noted that this definitive pronouncement was delivered by someone who had never once travelled outside Australia.

In any case the French national day began with a Frenchman in the yellow jersey for *Le Tour de France* and much speculation in the Press about whether he could keep it after tackling Stage 10 with its total of 7 climbs that would make it arguably the hardest day of the Tour. To further elaborate on that statement, the following details may help to put the demands of Stage 10 into perspective. The diagram below represents the series of tasks the riders faced.

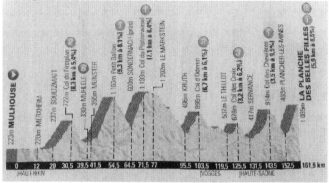

During the space of 161 kilometers (100 miles) the riders would face a harrowing series of challenging climbs, powered only by their own legs: 8.3 km (5.2 miles) at an average gradient of 5.4%; 9.3 km (5.8 m) at 8.1%; 7.1 km (4.4 m) at 8.1%; 6.7 km (4.2 m) at 6.1%; 3.2 km (2 m) at 6.2%; 3.5 km (2.2 m) at 9.5%; and 5.9 km (3.7 m) at 9.5% to the finish line in the ski town of La Planche des Belles Filles.

Unlike some laws which seem to be applied flexibly between one country and the next, the Law of Gravity applies equally to all *Tour de France* contestants – and in this case the battles on the uphill side of the gravitational equation would be very difficult.

The newspapers also reported that the leading contenders Nibali and Contador had decided not to attack their competitors on yesterday's Stage 9 because they wanted to save their energy for the difficult Stage 10 that was coming up. Full credit is due to Tony Gallopin for seizing his opportunity on Stage 9 to jump into the lead by almost a minute and a half while the other leaders looked around at one another and saved their ammunition. With all this anticipation the day's racing promised to be very eventful, and since it was France's national day the local papers reported that fireworks were to be expected along the route. Never let it be said that local press would let the opportunity to over-use a metaphor go to waste.

But before we could join in all this excitement there was a staccato shower to be taken in 30-second intervals. Upon entering my chosen shower stall I found that someone had left their shampoo bottle behind. When I examined the bottle I found it was labelled with the intriguing title of "Wash for Body and Hair", which made me wonder who the owner could possibly be. What type of person would need to use a shampoo for both their body and their hair?

Putting those thoughts aside we set off for the 80 minute drive to the mountain closest to us on the route, the *Col d'Oderen*. The papers had reported there had been more than 400 camper vans on one of the mountains in yesterday's Stage 9, and when we arrived we soon realized that a large portion of that flock of 400 had migrated to the *Col d'Oderen*.

While driving through one of the mountain villages we passed a man setting up a table for two in his back yard, complete with tablecloth. From this vantage point he would have a perfect elevated view of the route below, but it seemed like a very optimistic gesture considering the ominous grey skies above.

We planned to set up our van at a point 60 kilometers before the end of the stage, about halfway up the fourth climb of the day. However we encountered some difficulty finding a spot, firstly because many campers had arrived the night before in order to secure a place, and also because we arrived at 10.15am instead of our targeted time of 9.00am.

Eventually we created a place for ourselves on the side of the road on a slight slope, coincidentally two cars ahead of a car with an Australian flag on the windscreen. Making a mental note to go say hello to the occupants of that vehicle, we set up our advertising signs on the front and side of the Good Ship Gisèle - who had incidentally acquired a distinct list to starboard.

We sat and made breakfast as had been our routine but fried eggs were removed from the menu by the chef due to the ambient slope of the cooking surface. I was uneasy about the slope and got out of the van several times to check on the situation. Although the front right wheel had sunk a bit into soft mud, both rear wheels were on solid ground and I reasoned with myself that all would be well and we could simply drive out when the time came to leave, in reverse if necessary.

While I was reading the local paper after breakfast a couple of spectators walked by, read our signs and came back to the van to ask a question. It turned out that Robert and Janice were from the car with the Australian flag. They informed us that they were from Sydney and were in the midst of an extended holiday in Europe with their son and his girlfriend who are both living in Sweden.

During the course of conversation we learned that the family is staying in Mulhouse where the previous day's stage had ended. However they speak no French and did not know where to find the finish line so they could watch all the action of the Stage 9 finish followed by the presentation ceremonies. Describing the sequence of events from the previous day, they told us they had met a man on the street late in the afternoon just as he was exiting from an apartment building. They asked him in English about the *Tour de France* and he indicated with sign language that he did not know where to find it but that he would he call his wife on his cell phone. She was at home and came to the upstairs window to tell the man where the finish of the day's stage would take place.

In a random act of kindness from a complete stranger, rather than simply giving them directions the man walked with Robert and family for almost 30 minutes to take them to the finish point before simply saying "A*u revoir"* and walking away. This was an enormous gift to Robert who is a former champion cyclist and had always dreamed of seeing *Le Tour* in person. He told me how his mother used to often buy the French sports newspaper *L'Équipe* for him when he was young, and he would pore over the cycling pictures despite being unable to understand any of the accompanying text.

Later that night it was arranged that in order to secure place on the route of Stage 10, the whole family would get up at 3am to drive to the *Col d'Oderen* where it was that we happened to meet them. They had driven their rental car in pouring rain in the dark and had been parked since 4am, some 12 hours ahead of when the riders were scheduled to arrive. Not only were the unfamiliar roads and driving conditions hazardous to Robert, but this was also the first time he had ever operated a left-hand drive car.

He recounted one particularly memorable moment during the journey when he decided to overtake the semi-trailer ahead of him. The rain was especially heavy at that moment on the dark road, and being unfamiliar with European cars and their controls, just as he pulled out to pass the truck Robert accidentally turned off the windscreen wipers instead of turning on his indicator. At that same moment the windscreen was hit by the full force of the water being thrown up by the rear wheels of the semi-trailer.

Apparently Janice's scream awoke the young adults who had been dozing in the back seat and all paid close attention to the road for the remainder of the trip. His story reminded me of a bumper sticker I once read: "I want to die peacefully sleeping, just like my grandfather. Not yelling and screaming like the passengers in his car."

After their short night and harrowing drive Robert and Janice mentioned they were dying for coffee. We only had two cups in our van and after a while we took them each a cup of coffee and then later a cup each for the younger couple. My wife later offered the ladies the use of our bathroom which they gladly accepted while Robert and his son Pete erected the Australian flag on the side of the road using cable ties and duct tape Robert had brought from Sydney for this very purpose. It struck me that this level of organization and attention to detail was quite a contrast to me who had not even remembered to bring an Australian or American flag with me from Texas.

Despite not speaking French, Robert managed to start up a conversation of sorts with the French family in the vehicle next to him. I went and joined them and learned that they had driven over for the day from Nancy along with their son. I was tempted to ask *Madame* about her thoughts regarding the possibilities of future grandchildren given the status of her son as a Nancy boy, but I thought better of it. She'll just have to find out for herself. Sometimes life is hard.

I explained the concept of the Publicity Caravan to Robert, which was about to arrive and of which he had neither seen nor heard since it's such a localized event. It continued to rain on and off throughout the day, sometimes heavily, and it rained during part of the Caravan parade which contributed to the ungainly sight of the matron next to me falling over with her legs in the air as she reached to grasp a prize thrown from a passing float. In the meantime Robert and his family happily embraced and enjoyed the event along with the other spectators.

I had heard from Robert's son that there was a group of four young Aussies further up the hill from our position, and so I walked up to pay them a visit. I found them set up in style in a large white camper van with an awning displaying Australian flags on each side. The majestic location and arrangement of their encampment made it look like a traveling Australian Embassy rather than a simple camper van. Even though the weather was cool and rainy, to their credit they were doing their best to maintain a constant intake of fluids to avoid dehydration. I walked over to say hello, and was greeted by a young man wearing a navy blue toga. Perhaps the toga had been created from an Australian flag, but I felt it prudent not to make further enquiries on the subject lest my interest be misinterpreted as being other than academic in nature.

As we had expected, by the time the riders reached our position they had spread out more than we had seen on other days. Instead of one small group followed a few minutes later by one large group and one or two individuals, today we saw about five groups of 10 riders, one group of about 50, and about three groups of two or three individuals. Just before the final group of two, there was an individual rider from Orica-GreenEdge Simon Yates, riding all on his own. We cheered him on and he acknowledged our support while at the same time silently conveying the difficulty that he was feeling as he climbed the mountain.

These last few riders were clearly in pain yet they still had 60 kilometers and four mountains to crest before they would be able to rest. The time gap from the first rider to the last was around 20 minutes and we wondered how long it would be before those riders who were not skilled at climbing would make it to the finish. As it turned out, Simon Yates finished fourth from last on the day, 32 minutes behind the winner. However this was considerably better than the last two riders who finished 43 minutes behind the stage winner.

Meanwhile near the travelling Australian Embassy a 6-foot-tall gorilla wearing a Hawthorn Aussie Rules Football jumper was encouraging the riders, running alongside them for short distances and waving a large Australian flag. I was proud of his national spirit but I should later have walked over and told him where he could find his lost shampoo bottle. The toga man too was running alongside the riders and I applauded his willingness to sally forth despite the inevitable shrinkage issues that might raise their heads (or not) in such cool and damp conditions.

While talking with Robert and family after the riders had all passed, we realized that none of us had been able to spot Alberto Contador in any of the groups – even though we saw that one of the last groups contained a number of his teammates.

We later would find out that Contador had fallen and fractured his tibia earlier in the day on one of the descents, thus eliminating him from the 2014 *Tour de France*. The team had stayed back with Contador after he fell, and it took some time before he was able to remount his bike. He rode on bravely for a while before finally having to give up the battle. By this point Contador's team members found themselves a long way behind the main group of riders, with plenty of catching up to do.

Despite his best efforts and the emotional support of the entire country, the Frenchman Tony Gallopin was unable to keep up with the lead riders and finished in 33rd place on the day. Nibali won the stage in emphatic fashion, thereby regaining the yellow jersey and relegating Gallopin to 5th place overall.

Meanwhile a strong performance from the "bloody Tasmanian" Richie Porte saw him jump to 2nd place overall. I hoped the two Englishmen whom we had met earlier were pleased with the news, since this was quite an effort from a rider who had suddenly been promoted to team leader after the withdrawal of the race favorite Chris Froome.

As a former competitive rider who had long dreamed of witnessing the pinnacle event of the cycling world, Robert had loved every moment of the day and was emotionally moved by the spectacle to the point of having tears in his eyes as the riders passed him by.

After all the riders and cameras had passed, we removed our signs from the van and Robert offered to wait for us to leave in case we got stuck in the mud. He too had looked at the rear wheels and concluded as had I that all would be well, but he told us he would stay "just in case". I had had uneasy feeling all day but had overcome it with the rational thought that we could simply drive out of our location driven by the rear wheels that would push us forward. I got in the van to "simply drive out" and learned at this very inopportune moment that Gisèle had front wheel drive and not rear wheel drive.

In the process of trying to drive out we dug the front right wheel in even deeper and leaned closer to dropping down the adjacent embankment into the forest. Seeing our situation, Robert and his son Pete came to push but we were still stuck. By this time the stretch of road that had previously been crowded with cars and camper vans was completely deserted except for our two vehicles. With rising concern in my mind, I dug mud away from beside and in front of the front right wheel and in an attempt to improve the wheel's traction inserted some large sticks that Pete had found. I now realized too late that the constant rain during the day must have continued to soften the mud and caused us to slowly sink during the last few hours.

In a final attempt to extract ourselves, all three ladies were added to the pushing team and this time we slowly moved forward and got out of the mess with much relief all around. We thanked Robert and his family and hoped that we may meet again on the next stage. There had been no obvious need for them to have stayed with us, and I had even told them that we would probably be fine. Thank goodness for us that they decided to pay forward the random act of kindness from which they had benefitted the day before.

Much relieved, we were now able to make our way back to the campground - completely unaware that Geraldine had a trick in store for us. After initially telling us to head downhill and letting us proceed as such for about ten minutes, she abruptly changed her mind and instructed us to "turn around when possible". Not wanting to head back up the mountain into the sea of camper vans we continued on our way, climbing up and over another mountain and driving along some spectacular roads with steep drops that had my wife sitting motionless and white-knuckled. Fortunately I was able to find the right recipe to soothe her nerves back when we got back to "Boozy Lake".

CHAPTER TWELVE

HARDER THAN IT LOOKS

Up until this point the riders in *Le Tour* had competed against one another for 10 days in succession, spending a total of just over 42 hours in the saddle and covering almost 1,800 kilometers (1,100 miles) in the process. A total of 18 riders had so far withdrawn from the grueling race, including Orica-GreenEdge's Mathew Hayman who withdrew after Stage 10.

Recognizing the demands placed on the riders day after day, the organizers of *Le Tour de France* schedule two rest days within the three weeks between the start and finish of the race. The first rest day took place after Stage 10, with the second scheduled to follow Stage 15. During this precious time the riders try to allow their bodies to recover while they treat any acquired injuries, supported by team trainers, masseurs and medical staff.

We too took the opportunity of using the rest day to prepare ourselves for the next five days of riding the roads of eastern France. After replenishing our food and beverage supplies, we moved further south to a lovely campground in the lower French Alps in a picturesque setting overlooking a river and lake to the mountain range beyond. Driving to and from the race for the next few days would involve driving along the edge of spectacular river gorges some 500 feet deep in places. Such drives would not help my wife's nerves but at least the weather was now fine and warm.

The rest day also provided an opportunity to catch up on the local print coverage of recent developments surrounding *Le Tour*. There was of course much disappointment that the French rider Tony Gallopin had been unable to retain the yellow jersey on Bastille Day. The French press had expected fireworks on that day's stage and the front page of the sports newspaper *L'Équipe* managed to stretch the over-used metaphor one last time as it screamed with the giant headline "What Fireworks!"

More details had emerged of the events surrounding the forced withdrawal from the race of leading contender Alberto Contador on the day of the fireworks. It seems that he fell on a turn in a downhill descent in the rain, gashed his right knee and had pain just below the knee. While his teammates waited, the trainers strapped up his knee, gave him a new bike and he rode on. After a further 18 kilometers (11 miles) during yet another climb he found that the pain had become too much, so he reluctantly withdrew from the race. X-rays later showed that he had ridden those 18 kilometers with a fracture of the tibia just below the knee. Contador certainly displayed amazing courage to try to continue in the race, but the whole unpleasant incident could have been entirely avoided if he had simply opted to participate in *Le Tour* on camper van wheels instead of bicycle wheels. I'm just sayin'.

After our Stage 10 adventure on the mountainside, we decided to pursue a safer (and thankfully flatter) course of action for Stage 11 by going directly to the finish line in the city of Oyonnax in the Rhône-Alpes region. We parked near the finish line which was directly opposite the local Rugby Union stadium, of which the town is quite proud. The first thing we did was visit the closest McDonald's (which happened to be 50 meters from the finish line) because I wanted to use their Wi-Fi access to upload my blog from the previous days.

Along the way we had seen an advertising sign for another intriguing alternative called "Chicky World" that offered fried chicken and burgers, but alas the sign offered no mention of Wi-Fi.

We arrived at McDonald's just before 10am and thought we might as well have breakfast while we were there. However there was no breakfast menu whatsoever, and the restaurant was staffed by only one server who moved very slowly and seemed totally uninterested in her work and in serving customers. There were a total of 4 customers in the restaurant, including us, yet we waited more than five minutes for a cheeseburger. We asked for creamer for our coffee but to our surprise the server told us that coffee creamer is not among the range of available accompaniments in this particular establishment.

Meanwhile outside at the finish line of the race, several semitrailers had been transformed into double-story viewing and hospitality pavilions. Loud music was playing while

people had brought chairs and were starting to line up along the route five hours before the riders were due to arrive.

After a while we went back to McDonald's for a cold drink, having become unaccustomedly hot in the nice weather that was so different to that we had encountered during the previous 10 days. There were now more customers and staff in the restaurant than we had seen earlier but we soon found that a medium diet coke cost US$3.00, about twice the price of the same item in Texas. We had been surprised earlier in the day that a restaurant located so close to a major sporting event had not been taking every advantage of the opportunity to conduct thriving trade. But now when we learned the cost of a simple soft drink we understood the simple tactic involved: when prices are doubled, the volume of customers required to make a target amount of sales income per day is halved. And the lower the number of customers that must be served, the less hard the staff needs to work. While reflecting on this innovative approach to commerce and savoring every precious sip of our drink, we heard some American accents nearby.

On looking around we saw a group of about 10 American college students from Tufts University who were studying at a satellite campus near Annecy for several weeks. They were happily eating burgers and fries but I should have thought to tell them about Chicky World for their next meal. At the very least it would have been a good story to tell their friends back home, or better still their parents who would surely be thrilled to think that their hard-earned funds were being sensibly spent if they saw an expense for Chicky World on their son's credit card statement.

We returned to our van to rest for a while and by the time we returned to the finish area at 2.30pm we found the crowd had grown to become three or four people deep along the last

400 meters of the race route with three hours still remaining before the riders were due to arrive. The atmosphere in the immediate area was reminiscent of a family picnic in a park-like  setting with trees and grass all around, and with groups and families sitting on rugs and folding chairs. Vendor booths were sprinkled in between, more densely closer to finish line, selling everything from cold drinks to hot dogs and race souvenirs. We settled in on a convenient patch of lawn to watch the race on a big screen set up at 150 meters before the finish line.

A short while later we saw on the screen that the leader of the Garmin-Sharp team (American rider Andrew Talansky), who due to a sore back had dropped behind the main bunch of riders, was progressively falling further behind. Finally with 55km (35 miles) remaining in the stage he got off his bike and was guided by a trainer to walk over to a guard rail where he sat down, looking exhausted. There were two more mountains to climb but he looked spent and it was clear that he would have to drop out of the race. But a few minutes later to everyone's surprise, he got back on his bike and rode on. He looked very emotional and it seemed that he would go on for a few more kilometers before giving in to the inevitable. At this point he was already nearly 20 minutes behind the leaders. The TV cameras followed him on and off as he battled on, supported by verbal encouragement from the team car that accompanied him.

Meanwhile attention turned to the Frenchman Tony Gallopin who once again lived up to his name and galloped to the lead with some distance to go, eventually winning the stage to the delight of the crowd. Simon Gerrans from Orica-GreenEdge finished 5th, but Nibali retained the overall lead with Porte remaining in second place.

While we were waiting to watch the presentations, a group of five local dignitaries lined up on each side of the official stage. The announcer introduced them all twice while we waited, just to make sure we didn't forget just who was who.

Some straggling groups of riders arrived during the series of presentations for the winner of Stage 11 followed by the Yellow, Green, White, Polka Dot jerseys and the award for the most combative rider of the day. After the presentations were finally over, the announcer encouraged the crowd to wait for the American Andrew Talansky and cheer his courageous effort. A few minutes later he finally arrived, 32 minutes behind the winner, greeted by loud cheers from the crowd that appreciated the determination he had displayed. The press reported the next day that his Team Director had encouraged him for the sake of his teammates, trainers and the Garmin-Sharp supporters not to give up.

After hearing and seeing the efforts made by Contador and Talansky, I began to wonder if this whole bike race thing might be harder than it looks?

CHAPTER THIRTEEN

CULINARY CHALLENGES

Stage 12 started in the city of Bourg-en-Bresse, not far from the Swiss border. On our way out of the campground in the morning we stopped at the office to pick up the *pain céréale* loaf that we had ordered the night before. We expected it to be a rural type of bread and were not disappointed. It was a dark brown loaf richly encrusted with oats and grains.

When my wife went to collect the bread from the campground café, the server was not sure she was quoting the correct order, since it's an unusual type of bread for a non-French-speaking tourist to request. He was even more confused when he saw that the local daily newspaper *Le Progrès* was also part of our order. Somehow my wife was able to convince him through sign language that I could read French, and so he at last agreed with some reluctance to let her pay for and take both items.

We drove down to the start town on a series of mountain roads above breathtaking views of deep gorges surrounded by towering peaks.

I should add that I enjoyed the Alpine views much more than my wife who was holding on for dear life as we negotiated one cliff-side hairpin bend after another.

The center of Bourg-en-Bresse had been decorated in  celebration of the *Le Tour* and it offered many a postcard view. We drove on another 14 kilometers to the village of Neuville-Les-Dames where we parked Gisèle on the side of the road amidst agricultural fields just outside the town. Unlike our experiences a few days earlier in the mountains, we were now on flat land with ample space for spectators on both sides of the road, and most importantly were bathed in glorious sunshine.

A tractor arrived while we were waiting for the Publicity Caravan and my first thought was that it was a local farmer planning to make a statement of protest against all this *Tour de France* nonsense that was surely scaring the chickens and stunting the growth of his sunflower fields.

Three generations of a family group had already set up directly opposite us and were patiently waiting for the excitement to begin. However after a while the youngest member of the family reached the end of his tether and started to cry. He was soon cheered by the arrival of the Caravan but became scared by the passing Vittel truck spraying misted water on the crowd.

We had already garnered a stash of keyrings, hats, carry bags and numerous other items thrown from the sponsors' floats during the earlier stages but were still hoping to get a Carrefour tablecloth for our folding picnic table. It had been more than a week since we had last seen Carrefour car dispensing tablecloths but we continued to hold out hope.

While we were waiting for the riders to arrive I read in *Le Progrès* that saddle soreness is a common complaint among riders who are training before the new season begins. The body soon adjusts as it reaccustoms itself to the regular riding, but in the interim a commonly-used practice is to insert a piece of steak in one's riding shorts to provide some extra padding in the relevant area while on those pre-season training rides.

When the riders arrived we saw that rather than being used as a form of protest as I had imagined, the front end loader scoop attached to the tractor had been used by the farmer to create an improvised skybox for 3 spectators. Not the most  luxurious of skyboxes perhaps, but functional nonetheless.

The weather had now improved considerably compared to the start of our journey and we had started to make use of the outdoor picnic table and chairs that we had rented with the camper van. However the so-called "chairs" turned out to be folding stools that would be perfect in height and width for an 8-year-old, and so on the way home from the race we stopped

at a large mixed retail store to buy outdoor chairs. Naturally we had to buy wine at the same time because after all what good would a comfortable chair and table setting be without a bottle of wine to set on the table?

After finding two suitable comfortable folding chairs, to complete the purchase we chose the checkout lane with the fewest people in it. There was only one person ahead of me, a middle-aged lady who happened to be wearing a headscarf in Muslim style, and she was just putting through the last of her articles when I arrived. My hopes for a quick checkout were dashed when the lady motioned to the cashier that she wanted to pay for her groceries by check.

However it seemed she didn't know how to write a check, so the female cashier cheerfully did the whole thing for her with a good-natured smile. This whole incident made me reflect on the laws passed not long ago for public security purposes in France that restrict women from wearing headgear that covers their face. There had been much debate about the law, but it was nice to see that at the individual level in this part of the country there was no discrimination or resentment in evidence.

By the time we arrived back at our campsite the weather had warmed up to the extent that we decided to take a dip in the pool at the campground. After refreshing ourselves in the water that was significantly cooler than our pool at home in

Texas would be in the middle of July, we went to the café bar to watch the final 45 minutes of Stage 12 on television.

Not unexpectedly, yesterday's hero Andrew Talansky had withdrawn from the race before the start. He had fallen a number of times during the race and was unable to go on carrying these injuries. I was excited to see the Australian rider Simon Clarke from the Orica-GreenEdge team alone in the lead, but the question as always was whether the lone wolf eventually be caught by the rest of the pack before reaching the finish line. Inevitably Clarke was caught, but one of his teammates Michael Albasini was able to press on and finish fourth in the stage.

Clarke said afterwards that he had set his sights on this particular stage with the hope of winning it. He and four other riders had broken away from the peleton ten kilometers after the start in a brave move during a stage that was 185 kilometers in length. Halfway through the stage two of the breakaway riders fell, resulting in one of them having to abandon the race with a broken collarbone. Shortly afterwards, the remaining four riders had stretched their lead ahead of the peleton to five minutes.

One by one the other riders in the group dropped back until Clarke found himself alone in the lead with 26 kilometers remaining in the stage. He held on to his lead as long as he could but was finally caught and passed by the peleton an agonizingly short distance of 5 kilometers from the finish line. He eventually crossed the line in 141st place, more than 6 minutes behind the winner. The fact that he lost 6 minutes of time over the remaining distance of 5 kilometers indicates that Clarke had really pushed himself to the limit in an effort to win the stage. He said afterwards:

"We really want to win a stage. My best chance to win is by breaking away so I had a big crack in the breakaway today. I had this stage in mind since the beginning of the Tour. It didn't work out but the Tour is not over yet. We'll keep trying."

It's hard to imagine the level of effort it would take for a rider to win a stage such as this, where the breakaway riders tried to stay away from the chasing pack of hounds for 175 kilometers. Not only would the physical demands be immense but also the mental strain of knowing that there are some 180 people following behind who will work together as needed to foil the ambitions of the breakaway. However in recognition of Clarke's outstanding performance on the day he was awarded the prize for Most Combative rider for Stage 12.

Turning our minds back to more leisurely pursuits, my wife and I had been planning for a couple of days to have dinner that evening at a nice restaurant across the river from the campground. We arrived to find it all set up with elegant tables both inside and outside but with no diners in sight. After we had parked our van and were walking towards the building, the hostess emerged to inform us that the restaurant was fully booked for a function of some kind. As we left to go elsewhere we saw the first of the well-dressed guests starting to arrive. "Ok" we thought "we'll just go to that little café we saw in Matafelon-Granges near the campground".

The café was next to an old stone church that was now, due to declining attendance, served by a regional priest who says Mass there only the 1st Saturday of the month at 5pm. We parked and sat outside at a vacant table in an area that was about half-full. The waiter arrived a few minutes later and asked if we had a reservation, which of course we did not. He told us that the café was fully booked, although we could not see signs or even place settings on any of the vacant tables.

We gave up and went back to campground café, hoping that they were still serving dinner. Fortunately we were not too late for the kitchen and my wife ordered the chicken brochette (delicious) and I ordered the grilled entrecôte (extremely tough and almost entirely unchewable). Personally speaking, this was the second-worst meal I had ever eaten in all of my trips to France. I had experienced a more unpalatable event some years earlier in a seaside café on the south-west coast where I was lured by a blackboard sign the promised *bulots frais*. I was unfamiliar with the word "*bulots*", but the word "*frais*" told me that whatever these seafood delicacies might be, they were fresh.

There were four of us in the group and I managed to persuade everyone to order this special meal of freshly caught bounty from the sea. It wasn't until the meal was served that I learned that we had ordered sea snails, and they were prepared in simple fashion by being boiled and then served whole, shells and all. The vision on the plate was like a scene from my grandmother's garden in which snails would congregate around her geranium plants. And the texture of the flesh of these "delicacies" reminded me of my younger days when I played football and used a rubber mouthguard. The only difference was that the mouthguard was softer than the "fresh" *bulots* – I guess I should have been grateful the waiter hadn't served me stale ones.

CHAPTER FOURTEEN

STREET ART AND THE AIR GUITAR

On the morning of Stage 13 my wife and I both awoke with a slightly sad feeling to think that our remaining days in France were numbered. It had been two weeks to the day since we had arrived in Paris and in a little more than a week from now we would be heading back to the United States, leaving the joys and wonders of France behind us. We had joined *Le Tour* at Stage 4 and were now about to witness Stage 13 of the 21 that comprise each year's race.

As we had done the day before, we stopped on the way to the race at McDonald's to use their Wi-Fi system to upload the latest edition of my blog. It must be said that McDonald's restaurants are few and far between in France, and therefore it requires no small amount of determined effort to find a set of the famous golden arches in the more distant corners of the country.

Geraldine our GPS navigator, perceiving herself to be above such vulgarities of facilitating our eating at American hamburger restaurants, refused to offer any assistance in such a search. However being made in America, Siri the Apple iPhone wizard had no such qualms. She safely and efficiently took us to our nearest McDonald's – even though she pronounced it by spelling it out as M.C. Donald's.

Although from the outside this particular location looked similar to many McDonald's installations in the US, the existence of a well-stocked *patisserie* (pastry) section inside and the standard of customer service combined to provide a complete contrast to our experience in another location a few days earlier.

By now we had come to realize that the claims made by campground operators of offering Wi-Fi service to their residents are often greatly exaggerated. For example, at our most recent location the Wi-Fi access ostensibly offered by the campground was in fact a free 2-day trial of Wi-Fi offered by the local telephone company that just happened to have a cell phone tower nearby. If it had rained while we were there, I'm sure the campground operator would have bragged about the free car wash service that he had arranged.

After concluding my freeloader surfing at McDonald's we skulked out to the van, hoping no-one would recognize us as visitors from America and get the impression that we spent our entire vacation in France skipping from one set of golden arches to the next because of our addiction to American-style hamburgers. Of course nothing could be further from the truth – we were addicted to American-style Wi-Fi, not American-style hamburgers.

Now that our unpleasant little diversion was ended Geraldine emerged from her huff and deigned to guide us to the cute little town of La Frette, situated at about the midpoint of the day's route of 198 kilometers, where we would watch Stage 13 surrounded by an enthusiastic group of local residents.

While we were waiting for the Publicity Caravan to arrive a car from the Orica-GreenEdge cycling team pulled up and parked right behind us. This was the first and only Australia-based team ever to have entered *Le Tour de France* and naturally I was excited to talk with the two occupants of the vehicle. Apparently they had spotted the nearby bakery and had stopped for a quick bite of lunch. So far the results achieved by the team in its 3rd appearance in *Le Tour* had not matched the high standards it had set in the previous year when it held the yellow jersey for several days, but we remained hopeful that one of the team riders might win a stage before returning to Paris for the finale of the race.

I spoke with the two young men who emerged from the car and commiserated with them on the bad luck they had encountered when they lost the promising young rider Michael Matthews to injury on the eve of the Tour. On their return from the bakery, the driver gave me an inflatable Orica-GreenEdge "air guitar" as a souvenir.

By way of explanation I should point out that the team and its organization prides itself on its relaxed culture which has included the production of a number of light-hearted videos where team members and staff sing along to popular songs, simultaneously playing imaginary electric guitars. I happily inflated said instrument and taped it to Gisèle's windshield. For a moment I thought I felt her shudder at the thought of being decorated with an object of this nature, but it must have been a passing gust of wind.

Just prior to our surprise visit from the Australians the local residents, who were set up opposite us at a long table  displaying every intention of making a day of the event, painted signs on the road to encourage their two favorite French riders Thibaut Pinot and Romain Bardet. This effort was led by an ample matron who perspired in the 90-degree sunshine as she refined the details and nuances of her artwork to make sure it looked just so.

I would have thought that there was only so much refinement that could be added to the simple exhortations of *"Allez Pinot!"* (Go Pinot!) and *"Allez Bardet!"* (Go Bardet!) spray painted in large letters on a roadway but *Madame* clearly had a more discerning eye for the aesthetics of the situation than I. All I could do was stand back and watch in awe as she painted each of her letters in a thin blue line followed by the master stroke of adding a thin yellow line two inches away from each blue line, so that each letter was now written in both blue and yellow. I could only imagine the joy of the residents of La Frette who would now have the opportunity to enjoy this eloquent and imaginative expression of art on a daily basis for the next few years as they traversed the main street of their town.

When the Publicity Caravan arrived, a handful of the *artiste's* compatriots crossed the road and found an empty place next to us in order to improve their chances of scoring some prizes from the generous sponsors. One young man around 20 years of age was particularly enthusiastic in yelling *"Allez!"* (Go!) to every vehicle that went past, and thus we were treated to an almost constant stream of *"Allez Carrefour!"*, *"Allez McCain's!"*, and even *"Allez La Police!"* when a police car passed by. When there were simply too many different vehicles present to keep up with,- he resorted to the more generic but no less strident *"Allez! Allez! Allez!"*

He and his cohorts were accumulating quite a pile of prizes behind them as the Caravan passed and they grew ever more excited and raucous.

One particular lady in their group who was caught up in the moment went around to the front of our van and retrieved the Orica-GreenEdge air guitar from where I had it taped to the windscreen. She made a great show of it to her friends and family across the street as she brought it back to her excited bunch of supporters. The people across the street tried gently to inform her that this particular was not a random giveaway that she could claim for herself. They looked at her and back at me, and she looked at them and then back at me.

All of us were smiling good-naturedly as she pretended to play the guitar for the next float in the Caravan. I was prepared to let her have fun with it during the passing of the Caravan, but then she turned and added the guitar to her pile of prizes.

At this point I realized that she really thought it was hers, so I went and retrieved it and placed it inside the van on the front dashboard. It was a slightly awkward moment, but my friends who know me best will readily vouch for my long-standing interest in playing the air guitar. They will also be the first to agree that I have a great face to be on radio.

The riders all looked comfortable when they passed through the town, and Messieurs Pinot and Bardet managed to keep their composure under what must have been very emotional circumstances when they saw the moving tribute to them enshrined on the bitumen.

The race leader Vincenzo Nibali was well positioned with his team surrounding him and it appeared that most riders were conserving their energy for the final two climbs of the day which awaited them 20 kilometers further along the road. The first was to be 14 kilometers long at an average gradient of 6.1%, and the second a particularly challenging 18 kilometers to the finish line at 7.3% which included one section with a thigh-destroying gradient of 11.3%.

Richie Porte had started the day in second place more than two minutes behind Nibali, but on the final climb he was not able to match the pace of the leaders who rode away from him with 10 kilometers left to the finish line. He also reported stomach problems and lost almost 9 minutes on the day, dropping him back to 16th place in the overall standings. Porte was reportedly very disappointed with the day's results but he had represented his team well up until this point in the race by taking on the role vacated by the injured Chris Froome. To the undoubted chagrin of my two English acquaintances from a few days earlier, after Stage 13 Porte fell from contention in the overall race standings and eventually finished in 23rd place in *Le Tour*.

Nibali meanwhile rode alone into the lead of Stage 13 with just over 3 kilometers remaining, winning the stage and increasing his overall lead in *Le Tour* to more than three minutes. Thanks no doubt to the stylish roadway paintwork, the newly-crowned idols of the town of La Frette acquitted themselves very well with Pinot and Bardet finishing in 5th and 7th places respectively. Pinot moved to 4th place overall and Bardet to 3rd, with only 16 seconds separating the two young riders after 57 hours on the road spread over 13 stages.

Meanwhile Nibali's strong showing in Stage 13 confirmed him as the strong favorite to win the overall race, barring accident or injury.

After the riders had passed us by we climbed back up the mountain to our campground where we sat out in our new chairs in the early evening sunshine next to a clear mountain stream flowing through wildflowers and flourishing greenery. My wife cooked a wonderful dinner on the stovetop in the camper van and we dined outside on an omelet made with fresh local mushrooms, olives, feta cheese and mussels, accompanied by wine and a salad of fresh lettuce and tomatoes. Dessert  was local peaches and cream served with madeleine pastries that we had received earlier that day from one of the sponsors of the Publicity Caravan. Meanwhile on the hill opposite, a group of about 20 beige-colored cows lazily ambled home for the evening following the sound of the bell worn by one of their number. Perhaps it was the wine, but it felt like we were on the set of The Sound of Music.

It was a perfect and peaceful  end to an eventful day in rural France, and the setting was almost enough to inspire the composition of a new symphony for air guitar. However I don't think it would suit Julie Andrews' voice.

CHAPTER FIFTEEN

BEWARE THE PANAMA HAT

Navigating to a suitable vantage point for viewing Stage 14 required us to travel back down the mountain with my wife sitting rigidly in the passenger seat and keeping her eyes firmly focused on the road as we negotiated each turn, and allowing herself only minimal enjoyment of the spectacular Alpine views that I was trying to point out to her.

By way of indicating how high our campground was located in the French Alps, we were more than two thousand feet in elevation above the city of Grenoble which was the site of the 1968 Winter Olympics and also the starting point of Stage 14.

The race organizers in their wisdom arranged that today's stage would move directly away from our temporary home at the campground, and thus we endeavored to find a viewing point that was not too far past the start line. After our by now obligatory stop at the nearest McDonald's we chose the town of Vizille as our base for the day, and found it to be the most charming little town endowed with a number of well-preserved buildings in the center of the town and what seemed like more than its fair share of restaurants, many with outdoor seating.

We found a parking lot along the route close to the edge of the town center and settled in with our coffee and breakfast while waiting for the Publicity Caravan to arrive. While we noted that there were some decorations in the streets, there were generally fewer than we had seen in the locations we had visited earlier in our journey with *Le Tour*. Although the number of decorations seemed to have diminished to some extent as each day gave way to the next, the high levels of enthusiasm among the spectators along the routes had not shown any signs of subsiding.

At the appointed and well-publicized time that was printed in every newspaper the vehicles in the Publicity Caravan arrived, albeit slowly, proceeding carefully downhill into the town due to the right turn they had to negotiate soon afterwards. We had observed throughout the past weeks that some children seemed to love the whole event from start to finish, while others were frightened by certain characters. Some of the youngsters who came to watch the action were quite young, so one can just imagine for example the reaction of a bored and tired little girl who has fallen asleep while waiting and then wakes up to find the first thing she sees is a 10-foot-tall yellow cyclist looming directly above her.

And there are also other imaginative floats that probably look great on paper but are less practical when it comes to driving them for 120 miles each day up and down hills over roads both wide and narrow.

For example I am always captivated by the sheer quaintness of the little round mobile huts sponsored by Courte Paille restaurants. I'm sure they must have been designed by someone who either failed high school physics or at least fell asleep during the part about at the concepts of balance and center of gravity. It would be remiss of me not to point out at this juncture that *courte paille*, the name of the restaurant chain that sponsors these unlikely-looking objects translates to "Short Straw" in English.

I was not privileged to view the interior of any of the intriguing little contraptions but it would not have surprised me to see that each one of them was powered Fred Flintstone-style by a sturdy man using his bare feet for both propulsion and braking.

Nevertheless it was always intriguing to watch these extraordinary objects scuttle and scoot around the roads while I waited with camera poised to watch one of the circular little beetles overturn and go rolling down the nearest hill.

Speaking of bugs, the French version of the mass-produced small car is epitomized by the fleet (or swarm, perhaps) of vehicles employed by the sponsor and dry sausage manufacturer Cochonou. Their distinctive red-and-white gingham fashion style is reflected in the hats they distribute exclusively only to the most fashion forward fans in the crowd.

During the interim period while waiting for the riders to arrive after the Caravan had passed by we walked into town in search of a restaurant for lunch. Part way along our walk I realized that I had left my wife's Mac computer on the table in the van, clearly visible through the window. I was worried about possible theft and so I was anxious to get back to Gisèle despite the tempting array of open air bistros where we could have lingered over lunch. As it turned out we found a little pastry shop that was displaying in its window an offer for a takeaway lunch menu with sandwich, drink and pastry.

Once inside, we found our server to be a charming young lady of about 16 who was dressed in traditional costume and was determined to practice her English in response to me practicing my French. Her mother the pastry chef could be seen in the back room working on the next round of the daily production cycle, and upon hearing our conversation she offered to help her daughter.

The daughter turned to her mother and asserted her independence in a very sweet manner (I make this point only because during my life I have witnessed many teenagers, including myself, asserting their independence in a much less polite fashion), when she said *"Maman! Non! Sssh!"* then turned back to us. It was a lovely moment of a teenager taking a step out from under her mother's protective wing but not in a disrespectful way.

She completed the transaction with us and we took our lunch back to the van where we found that my feared invasion by mysterious thieves had not occurred. We had both chosen the dry sausage sandwich (perhaps made by Cochonou) on a delicious and crunchy baguette. For her dessert my wife had

chosen a very tasty lemon tart while I had a blackberry tart with whipped cream. It was a wonderful meal and we enjoyed every mouthful, even thought we were almost reluctant to disturb the works of art that were our dessert pastries.

The bright yellow filling of my wife's lemon tart was reminiscent of the *Tour de France* leader's yellow jersey which led me to reflect further on the current wearer, namely the Italian rider Vincenzo Nibali. He had so far disappointed me by refusing to wear the full yellow suit that I have seen race leaders wear in prior years, instead wearing only a few panels of yellow on his jersey. Even though he looked like being the winner of this year's Tour, he still looked to me more like just another member of the Astana team in their pale blue colors when what I really wanted him to look like was Tweety Bird on wheels.

As the riders drew closer and anticipation grew within the crowd, my wife noticed two little girls on the other side of the road who seemed to be holding an Australian flag. Naturally I was intrigued by the sight so I crossed over and spoke to them in Australian English - but there was no response from either of them. After a few moments I figured that they didn't speak English and so I looked into the crowd to see who their parents might be. Once again no-one responded. No-one that is except for a stern-looking French lady in the crowd who glared back at me. I figured that these two little sweethearts  aged about 5 and 7 must have been holding the flag for someone else, and decided it was best to go back to the other side of the road while I tried to turn invisible before the stern French lady called the Gendarmes about this older man who was approaching little girls at random.

Not long after this there were a few signs held up in the crowd behind the girls such as "G'day", "Tassie" and "Tumut". I clung to the idea that there must be some Australians on that side of the street but was not brave enough to go back for the fear of being arrested as some kind of stalker of unaccompanied minors. (However I must also admit that I was wearing a panama hat, which in itself has often been seen as an indicator of guilt in any given situation - for example, Sidney Greenstreet in several Humphrey Bogart films).

After the riders had passed by we crossed the street and were happy to see the two little girls together with four adults. As we walked towards them the same French lady from earlier was crossing the street in our direction and she gave me another disapproving look just for good measure. After finally making it to the other side unencumbered we had the pleasure of finally meeting the parents of the children, who turned out to be a lady from the Albury-Wodonga area in Australia and her French husband who happened to be wearing a cap with a New Zealand flag.

We were interested to hear that the family lives in the area near today's stage, and that the other two adults in the party were the Australian lady's parents who were visiting from Australia for about 6 weeks. Of course we congratulated the Aussie lady (whose name we forgot to ask) on her foresight in arranging for the passage of *Le Tour de France* near her home to coincide with the visit of her parents. We found that the girls did indeed speak English but were both rather shy in nature. It was nice to talk with them all and we wished we might have had more time to chat.

It was interesting to note that we had not met any American cycling fans up until this point of our journey apart from the group of summer semester students at McDonald's. There were 9 Americans entered in this year's race, 10 Australians, 4 Britons and 2 Canadians. We had met spectators from all of those countries except the US. Later on we would meet a number of Norwegians who were following the lone rider from that country.

While I was well aware that the popularity of cycling in the US had fallen significantly since the doping scandals of recent years, it was disappointing to think that so many Americans did not think it worth their while to come to the world's most popular country for tourism and watch the finely-tuned athletes in the world's premier cycling event. Not to mention the food, the wines and the fabulously elegant hats designed exclusively for Cochonou!

CHAPTER SIXTEEN

LIGHT AT THE END OF THE TUNNEL

For Stage 15, the race action was scheduled to relocate southwards from the Rhône-Alpes to the lower altitudes and generally warmer climate of Provence. Correspondingly, this also meant that my wife and I would have to leave behind our campground in the Alps with its mountain stream and picture-book belled cows to relocate to a new campground in the drier and flatter plains of the south.

For our new lodging we had chosen a campground in the Vaucluse region of Provence, which was an area I had visited a number of times over the past 15 years or so. We were looking forward to finally arriving in a warmer climate, but first there was the matter of driving some four hours to reach our new destination.

The first part of the trip called us, following Geraldine's advice, to drive down from the mountains on roads that were even more hair-raising than any of those we had experienced up until this point. The road we encountered on the first part of first part of the journey can only be described as a tribute to the determination and engineering skills of the civil works organizations in that part of France.

We began by passing under an arch across the road festooned with dramatic-looking signs sternly warning us not to proceed any further into the coming 20 kilometer stretch of roadway if the height of our vehicle was greater than 3.2 meters. We had been instructed in Paris that Gisèle's limit in this regard was 2.8 meters, and thus we duly ignored the road signs depicting cartoonish trucks looking as if they were crashing into a bridge as well as the other signs that showed cartoon trucks falling off the edge of the road.

The underlying reason for the abundance of warning signs soon became evident when we encountered the first tunnel on the route. Speaking of cartoons, this low tunnel looked like it had been that had built by an animated giant using an enormous jackhammer. The profile of the aperture through the mountainside was roughly elliptical and the walls and roof were unfinished rough stone. Just before entering the tunnel we had been driving on a country road with one lane in each direction clearly delineated by a center line, and with a drop on the left side of about 20 feet to a stream running parallel with the road.

Upon exiting the tunnel after about 200 yards we found ourselves on a narrow road about 1½ lanes wide, with occasional small culverts dug into the side of the mountain to allow vehicles coming from opposite directions to pass one another. More importantly, especially for my wife, the drop on the left side of the road had now increased in depth to well over 200 feet and grew steadily as we proceeded along the road which seemed to have been blasted out of the side of the mountain.

Fortunately for all concerned, traffic was very light on this Sunday morning although we still had to drive slowly because of the many twists and turns of the road as it followed the contour of the mountain. My wife was all but frozen in place in her seat but solidified completely when after passing through a few more giant-built two-lane tunnels we came to a tunnel that appeared to have been built by Popeye using a hammer and chisel.

This single-lane tunnel had room for one vehicle at a time and lacked the much over-rated convenience of internal lighting. With a deep breath – or perhaps hyperventilation on the part of my wife - we plunged forward into the darkness hoping not to meet any large vehicles coming in the opposite direction. Within about thirty yards the tunnel took a sharp turn to the right and we were able to see daylight at the exit some 50 yards away. With relief all round, we continued on our way on what suddenly seemed to be a very spacious 1½ lane road even though the sheer drop on our left must have been 1,000 feet or more.

In several places along the road it looked as if the builders had started to create a tunnel through a section of mountain and carried away in their excitement had continued on to remove the wall on the left side of what would have been a normal tunnel. In other words we were now driving underneath what looked like a section of mountain hanging above us, unsupported on one side. Needless to say, even though there was now plenty of space and light in these open-sided tunnels my wife level of anxiety was only increased by the vision of hundreds of tons of rock ready to fall on us from above and nothing but empty sky to our left.

After a few more twists and turns we finally finished our descent and returned wider and flatter roads which allowed my wife to slowly emerge from the state of rigor mortis that had engulfed her for the past 45 minutes. It was certainly an impressive engineering effort on the part of the builders to create a road through such a challenging geographical environment and I wondered whether *Le Tour de France* might ever feature this particular stretch on one of its stages. However the Popeye single-lane tunnels might be a limiting factor, not to mention the ever-present risk of a rider or two toppling over the edge of the road. Perhaps the riders could wear parachutes as a precaution.

Three hours later we had arrived in Cavaillon where we planned to watch the race, about two-thirds of the way along the Stage 15 route of 222 kilometers (140 miles). There were a few small climbs earlier in the route but by the time the riders reached Cavaillon they would have a mostly flat run for the remaining distance to the finish line in Nîmes.

After a very pleasant lunch of *Salade Provencale* while seated outside at a restaurant Place Leon Gambetta in the center of the town, we took our place among an expectant crowd to await the arrival of the Caravan. As was the case in almost every location we had visited, the parade by the colorful Caravan was a highlight for both the young and young-at-heart. In the distance we could see ominous dark clouds, but the Caravan passed us by in bright sunshine for which I'm sure the various workers seated on top of the floats were very grateful after the cold, wet and windy conditions they had endured on earlier stages of the race.

Quite near to us was a group of about 20 Norwegian supporters avidly following the sole Norwegian in the Tour,

Alexander Kristoff. It wasn't hard to spot them, given that they were all wearing matching t-shirts and waving small Norwegian flags.

The first riders to reach Cavaillon were like a pair of frightened rabbits being chased by a pack of baying hounds. The Swiss rider Martin Elmiger and the New Zealander Jack Bauer had broken away from the peleton within the first couple of kilometers and at one point their lead was around 9 minutes. Despite being on different teams, the two riders co-operated with one another to build their lead over the peleton. By the time they passed our viewing position with 65 kilometers remaining, the lead had been reduced to two minutes.

Stop me if you've heard this story before, but it looked like the brave effort by the two leaders would eventually be for nought as the peleton would inevitably catch up and then pass them about 5 kilometers from the finish line.

Bauer was one of only two New Zealanders competing in this year's race, and was a member of the Garmin-Sharp team that had lost its leader Andrew Talansky a few days earlier despite his gallant effort to try to stay in the race. Apparently the Garmin-Sharp team had met that morning and agreed that they would do whatever was required to have one of their riders in the inevitable breakaway on Stage 15. In other words, when Bauer flashed past us in Cavaillon he was not only bearing the hopes of his team on his back but also those of his countrymen watching the race live in the early hours of the morning, because the other New Zealander who had started the race had withdrawn after crashing during Stage 4.

Not long after leaving Cavaillon, the dark clouds that had been threatening to erupt finally delivered on their promise, saturating the field and making the roads more treacherous. Nevertheless Bauer and Elmiger continued undaunted toward the finish line, pursued by the baying hounds in the peleton who continued to slowly gain ground on their quarry. With five kilometers remaining to the finish the gap was less than 30 seconds as Bauer and Elmiger fought on bravely. By the time the valiant pair reached the start of the final kilometer, their lead was down to 14 seconds. A few hundred meters later, Bauer broke away from Elmiger and held the lead on his own as he battled toward the finish line with the peleton breathing down his neck. Fighting on to the last, Bauer did his best to sprint towards the finish line that was growing tantalizingly closer until the lead sprinters from the peleton caught and passed him a mere 25 meters from the finish. First across the line in a bunch finish was the Norwegian Alexander Kristoff, while Bauer finished 10th and Elmiger 16th. Michael Albasini from Orica-GreenEdge finished 9th, but in truth the riders were so closely grouped together that the first 69 riders to cross the line were all awarded the same time.

While the Norwegian fans we had met in Cavaillon must have been ecstatic, Bauer's reaction was quite the opposite as he broke down in tears after crossing the finish line. He commented afterwards:

"It's a childhood fantasy to win a stage of the Tour for any cyclist, and especially for a Kiwi cyclist. Not many of us get the chance to start the Tour de France. I really gave it absolutely everything, and as you can see from my meltdown at the finish line, I was pretty disappointed to come away empty-handed."

It was a cruel twist of fate for Bauer to have fallen short of his goal after leading the stage for some 220 kilometers, but he was so spent from his exertions that he was unable to get out of his saddle to increase his speed in the closing moments of the final sprint to the line.

For his part, Elmiger was more philosophical in his response and was pleased to have done so well after two grueling weeks on the road. He had not thought that he and Bauer would hold on to the lead for as long as they did, but called the second place finish of his teammate - the Australian Heinrich Haussler – "a super result for the team".

After the excitement of the race had died down we steered Gisèle towards our next campground, driving in the rain against the heavy flow of spectator traffic from towns located at earlier points along the route of the stage. Although we had stayed at a number of different campgrounds up until this point, we differentiated between each of them in our minds by recalling their unique identifying characteristics. For example, the one with no credit cards, the one with the mosquitoes, the one with the goats on the roof of the shed, the one from the Sound of Music and so on. This campground in the Vaucluse however would be remembered as the one in the forest.

Allow me to elaborate lest that simple term evoke a misleading picture in the mind of the reader. To put it mildly, it appeared that the owner of a few acres of land covered in oak trees suddenly woke up one morning and decided to go into the campground business. The major part of putting this inspired idea into action was simply a matter of bulldozing a few dirt tracks, sawing down a few strategically-placed trees and then *voilà!* a campground was born. But not just any campground – it would be a campground where the welfare of the trees would be more important than that of the campers and their vehicles.

Navigating along the narrow dirt tracks in Gisèle was hard enough given the trees on both sides of the track, but I pitied the owners of camper vans larger than ours. The individual lots were small and it seemed that as few trees as humanly possible were destroyed as part of the building process. In our case it appeared that the owner could not bear to entirely remove a particular individual tree located in the center of the lot allocated to us, and thus it was sawn off 6 inches above the ground to serve as a memorial to the tree that had once lived and to the underside of the cars, vans and trailers that had once been undamaged.

After finally maneuvering Gisèle into our assigned lot we soon discovered that the flow of water within the van was no longer working. We could hear the pump operating but there was no output at the sink or bathroom. As veterans of an earlier interruption to the water supply from our first day in the van, we surmised that the problem was likely a feeder hose that had become disconnected from the water pump. At the time that we picked up the van we had been provided with a list of dealers throughout France who could perform any maintenance tasks that may be required during our journey, and we soon identified a dealer located about two hours away.

I immediately called the office of that dealership and spoke to the owner in an effort to make sure that they could indeed work on our problem if we drove there the next day. While this gentleman was very cordial and polite, he regretted to inform me that his entire maintenance department would be unavailable tomorrow. When I asked about the following day he informed me that his maintenance technician was on vacation for the next two weeks. I guess even a department of one person needs to take time off every now and then.

Returning to the list of dealers, I found one in the city of Pau in the Pyrénées region who could help us after we travelled from the south-east to the south-western corner of the country as scheduled a couple of days later. In the meantime we would have to manage with large bowls of water for dishes and toilet flushes.

Fortunately the nearest water tap was within easy walking distance of our lot - the main problem would be to avoid tripping over the memorial tree stump along the way at 2am on a rainy morning.

CHAPTER SEVENTEEN

BUMP OVERHEAD

One of the unforeseen problems with parking a van 20 feet long in the middle of a forest overnight is that it can be rather tricky to extract oneself the next morning – especially if there is a tree stump lurking in the middle of the small amount of space available for performing the motorized gymnastics that are required to effect the desired extrication from one's closely-timbered surrounds. Adding further complication to the less than ideal situation was the fact that the ground underneath the vehicle was still wet and slippery from the day before. Nevertheless my wife gamely took on the task of providing directions, circling around the van and repeatedly marching from one end of the lot to the other to guide the process of leaving the campground lot.

Perhaps I'm making it sound overly complicated, but in reality a simple 15-point turn was all that was required to turn the van around so that we could drive out. We might have been able to do it in 11 points (with a mere 11 shifts between reverse and 1ˢᵗ gear) except for a certain tree stump that seemed to have the uncanny ability to constantly relocate itself to exactly where it needed to go to impede the progress of one wheel or another.

On the way out of Provence we stopped for breakfast in  Joucas, a lovely little old village set on the side of a hill with a glorious view across miles of vineyards, olive orchards and lavender fields to the Luberon mountain in the distance.

Although this was a rest day in *Le Tour*, we didn't have much time to linger and stroll through the alleyways because our packed schedule called for us to drive almost 500 kilometers west across France to the Midi-Pyrénées region so that we could check in to our new campground in Masseube before 7pm when the office was due to close for the day.

As it turned out, my wife did most of the driving while I sat behind her at the dining table working on my laptop to catch up on my blog and sort through the many photos we had both taken during the past weeks. The configuration of Gisèle worked very well for this purpose as I was able to remain seated at the table while wearing a seat belt, with a view through the front window so that I could offer road directions to my wife as needed.

Meanwhile I was also able to call the van dealer in the city of Pau, near the border with Spain, to confirm our arrangements for the next day when we hoped to have the luxury of running water restored to our living situation. This dealership was located about another 90 minutes further west from our new campground but we did not mind the thought of going out of our way in return for removing the necessity for late night trips to either the bathroom building or the nearest water tap.

The *autoroute* was full of holidaymakers, many of whom seemed to want to take everything *and* the kitchen sink with them. Some towed small trailers behind their car, while others found creative packing methods for loading up their roof rack, supported by the liberal use of duct tape. Fortunately for our academic purposes, the unavoidably frequent stops at toll plazas afforded us ample opportunity for the up-close study of the creative packaging methods of the French holidaymaker. We noted that bicycles of many shapes and sizes were a common fixture on the exterior of camper vans and cars, as were colorful plastic kayaks. Despite the often precarious methods used to secure the vacationers' worldly goods, it must be said that we did not at any point encounter any flattened bikes or canoes on the side of the road.

As we got closer to the Pyrénées the sunflower fields around us became larger and more numerous. Meanwhile excitement for *Le Tour de France* had been building in the region because the next three stages would take place in the general area. Some of this eager anticipation was expressed in the form of colorful pennants in the streets, some in the form of special color inserts in the newspaper, and some in the form of artful roadside sculpture.

After driving for most of the day, we finally arrived at our new campground. In contrast to the previous location where trees were the dominant feature of the landscape, the Masseube campground was a large green open space with lush grass from one end of the park to the other. Mature trees were planted throughout in a grid pattern with the rows about 30 feet apart. The trees were thus used to mark the corner of the camping lots, each of which was a spacious 30 feet by 30 feet. I noted with relief that the morning's complicated reversing and repositioning maneuvers would not be required in this location and neither would my wife's hand signals and directions. Best of all, there was not a tree stump to be found.

At the distant end of the park a small circus tent for a children's summer camp had been set up alongside a couple of larger tents that appeared to be used for communal meals for the campers. Small individual tents for the campers were dotted in between the larger tents. For each evening of our stay in Masseube it sounded like there was lively music and entertainment underway in the circus tent, but at the time we left each morning to watch *Le Tour* there was no sign of life among the campers' tents apart from an occasional bleary-eyed youngster making his or her way to the bathroom block.

Earlier in our journey we had witnessed groups of school-age youngsters arriving by bus to watch different stages of *Le Tour*, from which we inferred that summer camps are a popular diversion for the children of France. We had also noted a number of older folks camping with their grandchildren, an arrangement which we guessed together with the many types of available summer camps would serve to provide ample opportunity for parents to take a summer vacation of their own.

On the morning of Stage 16 the *autoroute* took us to the dealer in Pau where Gisèle was to receive appropriate treatment for her plumbing problems. Before any work could commence, the dealer in Pau called his counterpart at the rental depot in Paris to verify the details of our rental and to request permission to perform the necessary repair. They arranged between them that we would pay the Pau dealer for the repair, and would be reimbursed upon our return to Paris. While the dealer's staff went about their business my wife and I browsed around the array of new and used campervans that were displayed for sale. Many of these vehicles seemed too large and lumbering for the country roads in France, while others similar in size to Gisèle sported bunk beds instead of a double bed. One very interesting alternative was a vehicle about one foot wider than Gisèle and with more headroom - but fractionally shorter in length – in which the double bed was stored near the roof above the living area and lowered by electric motor when needed. Having the bed up and out of the way except when needed created more useable floor space, allowing for very spacious seating and dining areas and a shower cubicle with a door. All of this would be a vast improvement on our present situation in which head-bumping was a daily occurrence, you had to step outside to change your mind and the person using the stove had to move almost to the driver's seat to allow the other person to get to the tiny shared toilet/shower area.

Meanwhile the repair work was taking some time and lunch was fast approaching. By now we had become accustomed to the importance of honoring the daily lunch ritual, and just as we were about to ask for a recommendation for a suitable eating establishment there was a sudden flurry of activity as the manager came to tell us that our van was ready. Just as we had suspected, the problem was that one of the feeder hoses inside the water tank had become disconnected. Our guess was that the manager and supervisor who had replaced the pump a few weeks earlier in Paris had not secured the hoses are firmly as would have been done by a technician who was more accustomed to the task. Nevertheless we happily paid 103 Euros for the repair job, completed the associated paperwork and headed out the door with thoughts of Stage 16 dancing in our heads. We were happy to think that all of our problems were behind us.

A few minutes later while we were sitting in the van at the dealership while planning which particular town or other location we might choose for the day, the receptionist came out and asked us to leave because they were getting ready to close the gates while the staff all left for lunch. We looked up and saw a mass exodus from the building while the receptionist jumped on her bike and headed out for her chosen lunch spot. We quickly started the engine and set off because we would never be able to live with ourselves if we delayed these fine folks getting to their lunch. In our haste to leave the premises we failed to notice that the repair technician had left the main skylight raised in a fully open position.

I'll let Gisèle tell the next part of the story.

"Bonjour! First of all, I am happy to say that my internal plumbing problems have been resolved by a specialist located in the Pyrénées. When a lady reaches a certain age such problems can arise but I did not want to see anyone in Paris about this because, you know, people talk. However it would seem that one of the medical staff failed to close my scenic front skylight after the other procedures were completed, and of course those imbeciles to whom I have been entrusted failed to notice this small oversight. They followed the directions from my cousin Geraldine the GPS, which took me under a stone bridge with a height of 2.2 meters.

> Once again they failed to notice the sign on the bridge because they were too busy talking that funny language of theirs. With my striking and elegant height of 2.8 meters, disaster was inevitable.
>
> Not only did my front skylight shatter into tiny pieces, my other two skylights were also broken. But worst of all, I am now bandaged with duct tape, wooden dowel and tacky blue plastic.
>
> *Quel horreur!* I now find myself wearing a winter color in the middle of summer!"

By the time we had recovered from our careless and damaging mishap it was too late to make our way to the race route 100 or so kilometers away from Pau.

Stage 16 was scheduled to finish in the town of Bagnères-de-Luchon, which was hosting *Le Tour* for the 52nd time. Perhaps not surprisingly therefore, the town is often known by the nickname of the "Queen of the Pyrénées". The length of the stage was 238 kilometers (149 miles), of which the final part consisted of a climb of 12 kilometers (7 miles) up a mountain at an average gradient of 7.7% followed by a steep descent of 22 kilometers (14 miles) down the other side of the mountain to the finish line.

The day had begun with Nibali in the overall lead of *Le Tour*, 4 minutes and 37 seconds ahead of the second-placed Spaniard Alejandro Valverde. The two young Frenchmen Bardet and Pinot were not far behind Valverde and the American rider Tejay Van Garderen was in 5th place. A breakaway group of 21 riders formed about 75 kilometers after the start and at one point held a lead of more than 12 minutes over the peleton. However the numbers of riders in this leading bunch steadily diminished as they commenced the last and longest climb of the day, and by the time they neared the summit there were only four left in the group.

It was the Australian Michael Rogers who eventually won the stage – his first ever in *Le Tour de France*. Nibali finished 8 minutes after Rogers, but he lost no time against his main competitors and thus retained the race lead. However Bardet and Van Garderen were not so fortunate and they lost two and four minutes respectively on the day, dropping back to 5th and 6th places in the overall standings. Meanwhile Pinot replaced Bardet in 3rd place.

It had been yet another eventful day for Le Tour, and especially for Gisèle with whom we were due to spend another 4 nights followed by a drive of about 800 kilometers (500 miles) back to Paris to return her to her home base. During the days to come my wife and I would become more familiar with the artistic permutations offered by duct tape than we had ever thought possible.

CHAPTER EIGHTEEN

DUCT TAPE DYNASTY

While Stage 16 was the longest of the 21 stages in the 2014 edition of *Le Tour de France* at 238 kilometers (148 miles), Stage 17 was to be the shortest with its total distance of 125 kilometers (78 miles). But whatever this stage may have lacked in length was more than made up for by no less than four challenging mountain climbs over its final 80 kilometers.

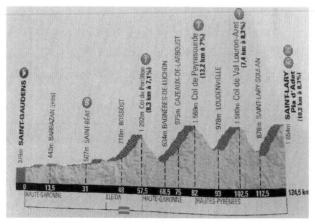

While a test was most certainly in store for the riders, in view of our earlier mishap in the mountains and the delicate state of Giséle's skylights we decided to observe this particular stage from a safe refuge near the town of Luscan. Not only would this decision place us 15 kilometers from the starting line on a flat section of road overlooking the lovely River Garonne, but it would also bring us conveniently close to a large hardware store with a good supply of the materials needed for improvising a solution to the drafty problems overhead.

Fortunately the weather had been sunny ever since our bridge-bashing incident, but there was still the forthcoming matter of driving some 500 miles back to Paris two days  hence. Based on our meteorological experiences so far, we were concerned that we would likely encounter rain at some point along the journey to Paris and it was our decided preference to keep such precipitation safely and harmlessly on the outside of the vehicle rather than dripping down the back of our necks as we drove.

But all of those problems could wait – first there was the matter of the Publicity Caravan followed by lunch. We continued to hold out faint hope for a Carrefour tablecloth, but the station wagon that distributed these delights of dining décor was nowhere to be seen. We had received a number of Carrefour riding caps, which are white with red polka dots in the same style as the King of the Mountains jersey and my wife's upper torso while in the Lille area, but alas the white-with-red-polka-dots tablecloth continued to elude us. There was nothing to be done but console ourselves with lunch while we waited for the riders.

By now we had settled into a routine of making a sandwich for our midday meal, based on fresh crusty bread from the nearest bakery with thin sliced ham, tomatoes, local cheese, mustard and *herbes de Provence*. Dried olives and small pickled *cornichons* served as garnish along with a glass or two of local wine. The intensity of the flavors in this simple meal compared to that to which we were accustomed in the United States cannot adequately be described but perhaps the following may help.

If a store-bought sandwich in Texas can be equated to watching *Le Tour de France* on a grainy 12-inch black-and-white television with a rabbit-ears antenna, then our van-made sandwich in France was the equivalent of watching the race on a 60-inch ultra-high-definition color cable television. In both cases the viewer is able to watch the race and know who won, but the experience of the event in one case is infinitely richer than the other.

We had originally thought that we would eat at restaurants or cafés daily throughout our journey around France, but dining out had become the exception rather than the rule after we had seen the enormous range of high-quality meats, fish, vegetables and other produce available in French supermarkets. Each day thus became an adventure to decide what to cook, and although I'm sure that not every meal was cooked to *cordon bleu* perfection, the wonderfully vivid flavors of the food more than compensated for any small oversights in the preparation process.

But speaking of the enormous range of products on display, there was another section in the larger French supermarkets that surprised me with its breadth. I made this discovery by chance after going in search of a small pair of scissors to trim my moustache while my wife was perusing the grocery aisles. After finding my way to the Personal Care section for men I was convinced I would find a series of choices of tools and trimmers for controlling the overgrown moustache perched untidily on the top lip of so many Frenchmen.

In this particular section of the store there were four display stands placed side by side, each with five shelves. However I did not find a single moustache kit or tool of any kind, which I guess would explain why so many French top lips remain gloriously unkempt and overgrown. What I found instead was shelf after shelf after shelf of men's after-shaves, colognes and moisturizing lotions. The only two shelves within this section that were not devoted to fragrance and skin care contained mouthwash and dental floss. I don't know what the relative proportions of the availability of these products mean in terms of the average Frenchman's philosophy towards personal care and grooming but I can only guess that an untrimmed moustache is useful for concealing one's dental defects, and fragrant cologne is often used instead of mouthwash.

Such concerns as these would have been far removed from the minds of the remaining 167 riders who started Stage 17 following the withdrawal of Simon Gerrans from the Orica-GreenEdge team. Throughout the race Gerrans had been suffering the effect of injuries he sustained during a crash on Stage 1 and although he was disappointed not to be able to continue all the way to Paris, it was decided that he would withdraw from the race and allow himself to recover fully.

The riders passed us at high speed in close to single file, with the race leader Nibali wearing his two-tone pale blue and yellow suit instead of the all-yellow outfit that I still craved to see. I would imagine that wearing an outfit like that would make one feel like a mascot for the Lemon Grower's Society but it would help spectators to identify  the race leader more easily within a fast-moving group of riders passing by.

The route took the field of riders into Spain just prior to commencing the first mountain climb of the day, and a group of 6 was in the lead when they reached the summit and crossed back into France. During the downhill descent that followed, the breakaway group of 6 was caught by a second group of 16 riders. But at the foot of the next climb, Vassil Kiriyenka from Belarus broke away from the group of 22 riders and in a remarkable effort rode up the next mountain alone leaving the peleton about five minutes behind him. He continued his aggressive riding and almost repeated his solo feat on the third mountain but was caught during the final kilometer of the ascent.

At the foot of the fourth mountain the lead group had been whittled down to four riders, with Nibali's group two minutes behind. With 9 kilometers remaining the Italian Giovanni Visconti jumped clear from the lead group and although he was eventually caught, he finished second on the day. Meanwhile Nibali made up a lot of ground on the final climb to finish in third place and extend his overall race lead by almost one minute. Only one other rider had been able to stay with Nibali during this all-out effort to the finish line, the Frenchman Jean-Christophe Péraud who remained in fourth place overall.

With the most difficult stages of the race completed, Nibali's overall lead was now an imposing 5 minutes and 26 seconds which meant he was all but assured of finishing *Le Tour* in first place. Most of the interest in the race therefore was focused on the minor placings, with the Spaniard Valverde in second position and the Frenchmen Pinot, Péraud and Bardet occupying the next three places. The American Van Garderen was in 6th position but 3 minutes behind Bardet and thus unlikely to figure in the race for a podium position in Paris.

In the meantime, my wife and I had our own race to Paris to contend with. After the riders and team cars had passed by our roadside location we turned our attention to the nearby hardware store to buy another round of wooden dowel and duct tape to construct our newest design for the large skylight in the center of the van. We had learned over the past couple of days that while the bright blue plastic tarp that we had taped over the skylight opening may have been impervious to water, it was not impervious to air traveling at high speed over its surface. Consequently the forces of highway speed travel caused the tarp to lift and stretch until it flapped noisily while it strained to work itself free of the silver duct tape holding it down.

A new design was needed for our makeshift repairs, and in the spirit of the expert engineers who used their ingenuity to make innovative repairs to save the lives of the Apollo 13 astronauts all those years ago, we set our minds to the task.

With a pioneering mindset and disregard for aesthetics that would have made the Beverley Hillbillies proud, we began by placing strips of duct tape side-by-side on both sides of the tarp to make it impervious to air. Our next step was to reinforce the underside of the tarp with pieces of dowel cut to length with a serrated kitchen knife. Together we hoped that these redneck repairs would allow us a quiet and uneventful return to Paris where we would have to confess our sins to the staff at the rental depot.

Fortunately for me, several large stacks of plywood had recently been delivered to the hardware store where they remained in the parking lot. This allowed me to park Gisèle next to the tallest of the stacks from which I could gain easy access to the roof of the van. Climbing on to the shortest stack and then on the next was much simpler than trying to climb the vertical side of Gisèle without a ladder. While I sat on the roof  applying duct tape to all three damaged skylights in turn, I noticed another camper van had pulled up in the parking lot not far from us. My envious admiration of its perfectly intact and pristine skylights was interrupted when the driver alighted from the vehicle and called over to me.

Vous avez une problème?

(Is something wrong?)

I wanted to tell him that all was well and I was simply climbed on to the roof of the van to improve my sun tan, but not only was I not in a joking mood but it also would have been unkind of me to respond to his genuine concern in such a flippant manner.

Oh là là! he said when I told him what had happened, as he winced and shook his right hand as if he had just touched a hot stove. Once again, as had happened on a number of occasions during our trip, a complete stranger had reached out to us with genuine empathy and kindness. Who said French people are rude?

After completing our "NASA meets Jed Clampett" repairs, our route back to the campground took us along a spectacular ridge with a valley on both sides leading to mountain ranges in the distance. The road took us through several small and charmingly picturesque farm communities with horses, goats and other livestock. It was while driving past one particular farmhouse that I encountered what I later realized was the potential epiphany of a lifetime.

Allow me to describe the scene.

On the right side of the road was a double-story stone farmhouse with a few large oak and poplar trees around it. The view across the valley from the farmhouse must have been spectacular, but that is not what caught my eye. Parallel to the road, in front of the farmhouse from our perspective was a large fenced pen of about 30 yards by 30 yards. Lush dark green grass covered the ground within the pen, but there in the center of the enclosure were two henhouses straight out of the Farmers' Almanac. Each henhouse was raised about 5 feet above the ground on poles, with a wooden ramp leading up from the ground to each henhouse entrance. The peaked roof of the henhouses completed the scene of what would have looked to me like poultry paradise except for one small detail – there were no chickens to be seen on the ground and it was too early in the day for them to be tucked up in their elevated quarters.

The answer to the puzzle appeared when I looked to the left side of the road and saw about 30 chickens patrolling another grassy enclosure, larger than the first but empty of any structures. Evidently the farmer practices free-range techniques and allows his chickens out during the day to supplement their diet with seeds, grubs and any other insects they may find for themselves. As I continued to drive I reflected on the lovely rural scene that underlined how close to the land a large proportion of the French population continues to live. It was not until about an hour later that I realized the opportunity I had missed.

Ever since I was very young I have been perplexed by one simple question that seems to recur frequently in my mind. Over the years I have heard many different answers to this question proposed by people from many different walks of life, and although each answer brought with it a unique perspective they were all somehow unsatisfying and incomplete. If only I had had the foresight to forget my petty skylight problems and park Gisèle on the side of the road for a couple of hours I would have been able to discover once and for all the definitive answer to the question that has plagued Man for generations: Why did the chicken cross the road?

CHAPTER NINETEEN

ONLY TWO MOUNTAINS

After 19 exhausting days on the road interrupted by only two rest days, the weary riders were confronted by the third and final stage in the Pyrénées Mountains which contained "only" two significant climbs. The first was to be 17.1 kilometers (10.7 miles) in length with an average gradient of 7.3%; and the second a grueling climb to the finish line of 13.6 kilometers (8.5 miles) at 7.8%.

Although Nibali held a commanding lead overall in the race, only 2 minutes and 8 seconds separated the second-placed Valverde from the fifth-placed Bardet. With the following stages expected to be significantly easier for the riders, Stage 18 offered almost the last significant opportunity for the rivals to gain time on one another – provided they were up to the task after already having traveled some 3,115 kilometers (1,950 miles) in the saddle.

The stage began with a group of 20 riders breaking away from the peleton and building a lead of more than four minutes over the remainder of the field. None of the leading contenders were in the group of 20 and as the first riders in the group crested the first summit of the day they remained four minutes ahead of Nibali and the other overall leaders. The peleton caught up to some extent on the descent from the first mountain, which meant that the gap was down to one minute and 15 seconds 12 kilometers from the finish line, shortly after the start of the day's second ascent.

Not only was Nibali able to overcome the deficit during the final 12 kilometers, but in a remarkable effort he rode away from the other riders to win the stage by a decisive one minute and ten seconds. In other words he gained a total of two minutes and 25 seconds on the stage leaders during the final 12 kilometers of uphill riding, resulting in an increase of his overall lead to a very impressive 7 minutes and 10 seconds.

Valverde struggled to finish 10th on the day and dropped down to 4th place overall, while Pinot and Péraud improved their overall positions to 2nd and 3rd respectively. The gap between 2nd and 4th places was now a mere 15 seconds, with Bardet in 5th place two minutes behind Péraud and Van Garderen in 6th, a further two minutes behind Bardet.

Nibali's series of impressive performances since gaining the yellow jersey after Stage 2 were regarded in some quarters as reminiscent of the days of Lance Armstrong and his 7 successive drug-fuelled victories in Le Tour de France. This brings us to the first of what I believe are two major reasons that interest levels in Le Tour are so low in the United States.

Many people, myself and my wife included, felt betrayed by the deception that Armstrong and his team had practiced for so long. We had both followed the path of his career from before his diagnosis and subsequent treatment for cancer and were thrilled to see him rise through the ranks to win his first Tour de France in 1999. As allegations of drug use arose, we ascribed them to jealousy on the part of his competitors who did not possess the same outstanding physical characteristics as Lance, who after all was a Texan!

As the chorus grew louder in subsequent years, we began to grow concerned when Armstrong would give indirect answers to questions about his possible drug use. For example when asked if he had ever used drugs I would recall his reply as something similar to "I have never tested positive for drug use." Nevertheless we continued to take his side in any discussion and pointed to all the great work he was doing for cancer patients through his charitable foundation.

The final revelations of consistent drug use came as a shock, but we could not let ourselves be angry with Lance Armstrong. Instead we focused on the thousands of lives he has touched in a positive way through his charitable work. Without winning the world's most challenging bike race seven times he would not have achieved the fame and notoriety that allowed him to launch his foundation and visit hundreds of sick children in hospitals around the world, inspiring them with his own recovery story. Having said that, he would not have won any of his seven titles without the use of drugs. This is not to say that the ends justify the means, but at least it can be said that there have been some positive outcomes from the whole Lance Armstrong saga, not the least of which has been an increase in the stringency and effectiveness of drug testing in cycling and many other sports.

Although this is the most recent high-profile doping scandal, there have been many others including the entire nine-man Festina team being expelled from the 1998 *Tour de France* after its team director admitted that he was conducting a concerted program to provide his riders with performance-enhancing drugs.

Not surprisingly therefore, the question of doping was raised with regard to Nibali – especially since his team manager Alexandre Vinkhourov had been banned for two years for blood doping during the 2007 *Tour de France*. However Nibali's Astana team is a member of the Movement for Credible Cycling, which is an organization that applies far stricter rules to its members than the International Cycling Union and the World Anti-Doping Agency which are the official watchdogs of the sport of cycling. Also in Nibali's favor is that his rise has been steady since he finished third in the time trial at the junior world championships at the age of 17, unlike several other riders from recent years who rose suddenly from obscurity, only to be later found guilty of doping. Before the 2014 *Tour de France*, Nibali had entered a total of 11 similar "grand tour" events of 21 stages and had never finished outside the top 20 riders. This included finishing third in the 2012 *Tour de France* and winning the 2010 *Vuelta a España* and 2013 *Giro d'Italia*.

If we can accept the circumstantial evidence that the most outstanding rider in this year's *Tour de France* is clean, then we can posit that the rest of the field must also be clean (or else using drugs that don't work!). This allows us to move on to what I believe is the second main reason for the lack of interest by Americans in *Le Tour* – there is presently no American rider with a good prospect of winning.

History shows that the first non-European to win *Le Tour* was the American Greg LeMond who won in 1986, 1989 and 1990, and was second in 1985 and third in 1984; while his fellow countryman Bobby Julich finished second in 1998. A total of nine Americans entered the race in 2014 with Tejay Van Garderen consistently maintaining a place among the top 10 overall standings and Andrew Talansky leading the Garmin-Sharp team until his unfortunate withdrawal. While it is true that there is presently no Greg LeMond ready to contend for next year's overall victory, there could well be a new American Nibali or Contador waiting in the wings while developing his skills to return the American flag to the podium in future years. Although it was largely overlooked by the media in the United States, the American rider Chris Horner won the 2013 *Vuelta a España* while one month shy of his forty-first birthday, leaving Nibali to finish second and Valverde third.

Simply because there is no American among the leading contenders is no reason for sporting fans not to follow the world's premier cycling endurance event and appreciate the skills and athleticism required to succeed. To refuse to take an interest in the race for that reason would be akin to refusing to watch the NFL Super Bowl simply because one's team was not playing in the game.

But three more stages remained in this year's Super Bowl of cycling, with 164 players remaining in the game after more than 80 hours of hard riding. As we prepared for our return journey to Paris, not for the first time I gave thanks for the fact that the wheels underneath me belonged to a reliable and sturdy diesel-powered camper van rather than a light and wobbly bicycle powered by my own all-too-fallible legs.

CHAPTER TWENTY

TIME TAKES ITS TOLL (AND VICE-VERSA)

In what seemed like an anticipation of our journey back to Paris, the skies opened up over our campground in Masseube in the early hours of the morning as if to remind us of the weather we had experienced during the first part of our stay in France. It was still raining when we arose early to start our trip of 785 km (490 miles) and the rain and lightning would stay with us for the first couple of hours along the *autoroute*.

While we were happy that our redneck repairs had kept out the overnight rain, we were concerned whether there would be any sudden surprises along the highway when the combination of the wind speed and rain would conspire to suddenly launch our elaborate skylight covering into space while simultaneously dumping a bucket or two of cold water down the back of our necks.

Not wanting to tempt fate any further, we decided that my wife would take the helm of Gisèle while I monitored the condition of the repair work from the inside of the van. After our experiences of the previous few days, we had planned to drive all the way to Paris at a speed of 80 km/h (50 mph) to reduce the wind speed over the vehicle. We had driven for about half an hour a few days ago with no cover over the front skylight and it was a noisy and uncomfortable experience that we did not want to repeat.

Despite these precautions I remained rather nervous about whether the duct tape would maintain its adhesion, but when we stopped to check on the situation after the rain had ended I was pleasantly surprised to find only one small spot where about an inch of tape needed to be pressed back into place. Even if our patched-up skylights had sprung a leak, I could at least assure my wife that I would never put her in the position that one unfortunate lady we saw on the *autoroute* found herself in, seated as she was in a motorcycle sidecar in the face of driving rain.

By the time were halfway to Paris, the rain had stopped and we had begun to relax and stop worrying so much about our duct-taped designs that decorated the roof of the van. Reflecting on the past three weeks we calculated that by the time we returned to Paris we would have travelled 5,000 km (3,100 miles) on the French roads, much of it on the *autoroute* system that criss-crosses the country.

Almost all of our *autoroute* journeys had required us to pay a toll of not insubstantial proportions; for example we had already paid around US$25 by the time we were halfway to Paris. The last time I had driven extensively in France was about 15 years earlier and at that time toll roads were few and far between. Apparently during the intervening years a large part of the highway system had been privatized and was now managed by companies who collect a toll to provide a return on their investment.

But for foreigners like us, paying up at the toll stations was not as simple as we might like. To start with, probably 95% of the toll stations we encountered were unattended and it was always a lucky dip to see whether our American credit card would be accepted or not. The European cards have an embedded microchip, whereas the American ones do not. As a result, using an American credit card at a restaurant or supermarket required us to sign a receipt. European cards used in the same circumstances did not require a signature.

If our credit card did not work at a given toll station, we would then have to fumble for change to insert into the machine slots which are placed at an awkwardly low height for those of us trying to reach out the front window of a vehicle such as Gisèle. For reasons only known to Signore Fiat who built the vehicle, Gisèle's front windows do not lower all the way to the bottom of her window frames but instead leave about 4 inches of glass that would have to be reached over to gain access to the toll machine.

Then if there were change to be dispensed by the toll machine, we would have to reach down to that particular aperture which has been placed inconveniently lower still. Even though I am more than 6 feet tall it was by no means a simple reach for me, but my wife had to get almost half of her body out of the window to perform these contortions. To her credit she devised a routine for this purpose whereby she would stop at the toll booth, put on the hand brake, undo her seat belt, lower the window, take a deep breath and gamely plunge into her task while I awaited her with credit card and coins at the ready – all the while remaining alert to the need to grab her ankles before they vanished completely over the window sill in case she leaned over too far.

After a while we became accustomed to all this fussing around, but one particular experience a few days earlier while on our way from Provence to the Pyrénées Mountains remains indelibly engraved in our minds. July is traditionally a month when many French families take vacation, and many of them choose to do so by car. The newspapers reported that at one point on Saturday July 15th there were literally hundreds of miles of traffic jams across the country caused by holidaymakers and their cars, caravans, trailers and camper vans. By the time Monday July 21st came around we thought that the holidaying crowd would already be happily ensconced at their intended destinations and consequently there would be no extra traffic on the roads.

We learned the error of our ways when we came upon a toll plaza that day in the south of France where cars, trucks, caravans and other assorted vehicles were lined up twenty-or-so deep waiting to pay their tolls. I counted 18 gates in operation at this plaza, of which only five accepted cash. The remaining gates were reserved for drivers using credit cards or the electronic tolltag system. These particular cashless gates saw very little traffic while the lines for the cash gates moved painfully slowly. I had chosen the lane that I thought had the shortest line when we arrived, but it seemed to be moving even more slowly than the others.

By the time we got halfway to the toll booth we saw that while there were five gates accepting cash, there were six lines of vehicles trying to use those gates – even worse, we were in one of the two lines that were trying to squeeze into the same gate. Finally after 30 minutes sitting and slowly inching forward, we got to the toll gate. Our credit card had not worked at any of the toll booths for the past 200 miles but I decided on a whim to try it anyway. *Voilà!* It worked. My wife and I sat and looked at one another. We had just sat through 30 minutes of unnecessary frustration when we could have gone almost straight through any one of the empty credit card gates.

No wonder the French take such long periods of vacation – they have to set aside time to get through the toll booths.

Although we missed watching Stage 19 of the race while on our way to Paris, time was to play a major role in Stage 20 which took place the following day. This second-to-last stage of *Le Tour* would follow a route of 54 undulating kilometers (34 miles) during which each individual rider would be timed against one another. They would leave the starting line two minutes apart and pedal furiously to the finish, unencumbered by other riders around them. For the three riders vying for a place on the podium in Paris, the time trial offered a golden opportunity to close the 15 second gap that still existed between the competitors in second, third and fourth position overall.

In particular Valverde, who was in fourth position at the start of Stage 20, only needed to complete the time trial three seconds faster than Péraud to jump into third position overall. And with a comfortable lead of more than 7 minutes, Nibali could afford to ride well within himself, secure in the knowledge that he would be crowned winner of *Le Tour de France* the next day in Paris.

Please stop me if you've heard this before, but rather than being content to maintain his overall lead, Nibali rode hard and finished fourth on the day thereby extending his overall lead by another 42 seconds to almost eight minutes ahead of the second-placed rider.

The American Tejay Van Garderen also put in an outstanding performance, gaining some two minutes over the unfortunate Frenchman Bardet who suffered a puncture late in the stage. Van Garderen would now move to 5th place overall.

Valverde on the other hand not only failed to gain three seconds against Péraud, but he lost more than a minute on the day and remained in 4th place overall.

Meanwhile Péraud had begun the day in third place, 13 seconds behind Pinot. Although both men performed creditably in the time trial with Péraud finishing 7th and Pinot 12th, Péraud gained 45 seconds against his countryman and jumped into second place overall.

All that remained was now the ceremonial final stage in Paris where the winners would be crowned during what promised to be a very special day at the *Champs-Élysées*.

CHAPTER TWENTY-ONE

LAST VAN GO IN PARIS

To describe the experiences of the last three weeks while living in Gisèle the ever-reliable camper van as simply enjoyable would be an understatement akin to describing Paris as merely an interesting place to visit. Gisèle had carried us in comfort and safety over 5,000 kilometers of *autoroutes*, suburban streets and single lane country roads. She had provided a comfortable travelling home for us and, despite our mishaps with parking in tight places and driving under low bridges, she had never let us down. Nevertheless it had still been three weeks of living in tight quarters and we were not sorry to hand her bandaged body back to her rightful owners upon our return to Paris and then check in to a hotel in the inner suburb of Fontenay sous-Bois. A full-size bathroom and a king-size bed were just two of the luxuries that we welcomed, not to mention the 10-foot ceilings of our hotel room.

We had informed the Paris rental depot about our skylight incident shortly after it happened, and thus the staff was prepared to take full stock of the situation after our arrival.

The manager who had helped repair the water pump problem three weeks earlier was on hand for our arrival, as was the supervisor who worked for him. We fully expected to lose the security deposit we had paid at the commencement of the rental period and were not surprised when the manager exercised this option.

However it was rather disappointing as a matter of principle when the manager refused to reimburse us the 103 Euros that we had paid to make right the substandard repair work that he and his colleague had performed three weeks earlier on the water pump. When I reminded him that he had agreed over the telephone with the dealer in Pau to reimburse us for the pump repair, he insisted that he had only agreed to reimburse us if the problem was that the pump was burned out. He then went on to complain about the price charged by the dealer in Pau for reconnecting the errant feeder hose, calling in his supervisor to get his opinion which naturally coincided with that of the manager. Although the financial manager seemed sympathetic to our plight, the depot manager would not budge from his position. In return, we made a mental note to exclude him from our Christmas card list. That'll teach him a lesson.

The final stage of *Le Tour* was scheduled for the day after our return to Paris, and although the racing on this day would not change the placings in the various categories of prize winners, it promised quite a spectacle as the route called for the riders to travel up and down the *Avenue des Champs-Élysées* a number of times before reaching the finish line.

Thanks to a program offered by the Australia-based cycling team Orica GreenEdge, we would be seated in a pavilion overlooking the *Champs-Élysées* close to the finish line as the riders travelled in a loop that would take them back and forth along the iconic avenue from the *Arc de Triomphe* at one end to the *Place de la Concorde* at the other. The 164 competitors would traverse this cobblestone paved loop a total of eight times, with each lap covering a distance of 3.8 km (2.4 miles) as we watched in comfort while reflecting on the symbolism inherent in the fact that the *Arc de Triomphe* was built to honor the victories of Napoleon Bonaparte.

Our first stop for the day was planned to be Mass at Notre Dame Cathedral, followed by lunch at a gourmet restaurant arranged by Orica-GreenEdge. From there we would watch the conclusion of Stage 21 from our seats in the pavilion. After much deliberation and scrutinization we had managed to decipher the series of train and Metro trips that would be required to make these plans come to fruition.

An early start to the day was called for, but the good news was that we would not have to put on sandals and bathrobe to walk 50 yards or more to the bathroom. Even better, once the flow of shower water had started there would be no need to keep pressing the water button every 20 seconds or so to maintain the stream.

We enjoyed a very special form of Mass at the Cathedral, most of which was in Latin and which was accompanied by glorious choral voices and organ music. During a pause in the proceedings I made a quick mental note to choose a Latin song for my next performance audition because no-one will ever know if I forget the words

– I can simply make up some sounds to fill the gaps and no-one will ever know the difference. As a matter of fact, I wonder if that's how that jazz form of singing called "scat" got started? Frank Sinatra probably sang "scoo-bee doo-bee doo" because he forgot the original lyrics. Who would have thought that a Latin Mass would help me solve a mystery that has been bugging me since my childhood? This was almost as cathartic a revelation as the chicken scenario from a few days earlier.

But as I was saying it was a very nice experience in the Cathedral and afterwards we walked over a bridge across the River Seine back to the closest Metro station.

"Paris at the Beach" was the theme of the month in this particular part of the city, where a large amount of sand had  been trucked in to the center of the city to create a "beach café" on one bank of the Seine and an even larger amount had been used to create a "beach rugby" field in front of the historic *Hotel de Ville*.

We paused for a few moments to observe the local rugby team players who were endeavoring to teach the skills of the game to passers-by. The problem seemed to be that the only passers-by who were interested to learn something about the game were all under the age of 10. Anyone older than that age would have by now acquired sufficient discernment to know that a game that calls for taking a perfectly good football and throwing it around instead of kicking it makes no sense at all.

The depth of the desperation to find a way to promote the game was further evidenced by the huge poster that defaced the façade of the historic building and advertised the upcoming "Women's Rugby World Cup". The poster featured a 50-feet tall woman dressed in loose shorts and a long-sleeve rugby shirt which probably had the effect of scaring some of the younger children away, while having no effect at all on anyone else.

I wanted to find the organizers of this Women's Rugby event and put them in touch with the management of the Lingerie Football League in the United States who could surely offer some helpful promotional ideas. Who would have ever thought that the Americans could give the French advice on how women should be dressed to attract more attention?

A few minutes later we were on our way to lunch and were sitting in a busy Metro car with all seats taken and many people standing, when the unmistakable strains of a saxophone rang out. But it wasn't just any saxophone; it was a saxophone playing Dave Brubeck's "Take Five". I couldn't see where the sound was coming from but suddenly I felt like I was in a Paris night club – albeit without cigarette smoke and a cover charge – and it created a pleasant and mellow feeling. This feeling was enhanced further when I realized that the music that I had assumed was entirely recorded was in fact provided by a middle-aged man playing a large saxophone together with the accompaniment of a portable stereo player to provide the backing track.

I did not feel quite so contented with myself when he passed along the carriage with a cup and I found I had nothing smaller than 20 Euros (about US$27) to offer him in return for his efforts. I hadn't realized that there were any musicians in the Metro but over the course of the day on our Metro travels we heard and saw very competent musicians playing the piano accordion, violin, clarinet and other instruments. It was quite atmospheric and a pleasant surprise.

After arriving at the *Champs-Élysées* we found ourselves on the wrong side of the street in relation to our restaurant. The road was completely barricaded in preparation for *Le Tour* and there was no way to cross unless we climbed the fence that lined the near side of the road and then talked our way past the gendarmes manning the route before climbing the fence on the far side. Although such an attempt may well have given us a story to tell our grandchildren as well as some interesting photos of my wife climbing a fence in her elegant yellow dress and high heels, we decided we would rather spend the remainder of the day as originally planned and not in the back of a van belonging to the *gendarmerie*. The sensible option was thus to go back down to the Metro and find an exit tunnel that took us to the other side.

When we finally arrived at the restaurant there was much confusion with our entrance invitation. When the well-dressed young ladies at the reception desk asked which company we were with we replied "Orica-GreenEdge". They didn't seem to understand that around 50 or so people under that name were due to have lunch in the restaurant. They refused point-blank to let us in while one of their number went to check with the management.

While we were waiting, an Australian couple with two children arrived and navigated their way past the fashionable gatekeepers with ease. The husband turned back to me and asked if we were having trouble. I explained what had happened and he replied that he would get it straightened out.

I thought it was very kind of him to offer and hoped that he might know someone who knew someone who could get us through the door. He had just introduced himself to us as "Shayne" when one of the event organizers arrived. He had a quick word to her and we were suddenly on our way in to the restaurant, problem solved.

As we were walking out to the patio for pre-lunch champagne I realized that this "ordinary bloke" who had gone out of his way to help us was none other than Shayne Bannan, who is one of the two Team Managers for Orica-GreenEdge. As if he didn't have enough on his plate after 3 weeks of *Le Tour*, it was very kind of him to take the time to step in and help us out.

Following the pre-lunch festivities we were seated at a table with a lively group of Aussies, some of whom had brought their bikes with them to France and had ridden portions of the race route. One Adelaide couple had even climbed the dreaded Mont Ventoux which frequently features in  *Le Tour* and which I remembered well from years earlier when I had traversed it in a small rental car, ever fearful that the engine would blow a gasket on the way up or that the brakes would burn out on the way down. To willingly place oneself anywhere on this mountain on a bicycle seemed like an act of courage that was well beyond the realms of contemplating running the gauntlet of crossing the *Champs-Élysées* on foot on the final day of *Le Tour de France*.

The three-course lunch at the Michelin-rated restaurant was wonderful, served elegantly by an efficient staff of waiters and waitresses who seemed to be invisible until suddenly appearing at our elbow just as we needed our plates removed or our glasses refreshed.

 After lingering over our post-lunch refreshments for a generous amount of time we eventually moved to the pavilion to watch the race. The riders were still in the countryside outside of Paris when we arrived, but a giant video screen on the opposite side of the avenue kept us informed of the progress of the yellow jersey and other members of the peleton. The arrival of the riders at the Champs-Élysées coincided with a flyover by French Air Force fighter jets trailing red, white and blue smoke. After passing around the Arc de Triomphe eight times, the final result saw the Frenchmen Péraud and Pinot finish respectively in second and third places which was the best result for the host nation in 30 years. Pinot also won the honor of the white jersey for the best young rider. Napoleon would have been proud of his countrymen as surely would the good folks of La Frette whose portentous pavement paintwork will continue to honor this year's 3rd and 6th place finishers for the foreseeable future.

As for us it was a day of sensory overload with a vivid and unique array of sounds, sights, tastes and aromas that could only be found in Paris. In other words it was a perfect ending to a wonderful trip.

LESSONS LEARNED

For those conspiracy theorists still trying to link Vincenzo Nibali to drugs, it was notable that his overall victory margin of 7 minutes and 37 seconds was identical to Lance Armstrong's winning margin in his first *Tour de France* victory in 1999 which was later revealed to have been achieved with the use of illegal drugs. Those caring to dig further into the record books would find that the average winning margin for winners (excluding Armstrong) of the 17 *Tours* of similar length held between 1981 and 2013 was 3 minutes and 38 seconds, less than half of Nibali's margin.

I prefer to think that Nibali's outstanding result was the culmination of many years of training that has produced results that have improved steadily over time in the international cycling events he has entered. He received strong support from his Astana Pro team throughout *Le Tour*, with the team finishing in 6th place overall. A review of my own photos of the different stages shows Nibali almost always surrounded by his teammates as they protected him from problems in the peleton and helped him conserve his energy for the latter parts of each stage.

Twenty-five days in France seemed to have passed by very quickly when it came time to board our return flight to the United States. We had enjoyed a series of unique experiences as we drove clockwise around the country, interacting with residents from different regions of France as well as fellow visitors from other countries who were drawn to the spectacle of the 101st edition of *Le Tour de France*. And I can think of no better way to spend next July than to follow *Le Tour* once again – this time as it traces its route anti-clockwise around France and showcases many more of the hidden delights the country has to offer.

Prior to leaving the United States we had resigned ourselves to the inevitable reality that we would both gain five or more pounds during three weeks of sampling the irresistible culinary delights that France had to offer, not to mention the wines and of course my particular post-prandial pleasure, Calvados. It was thus with much trepidation that my wife and I stepped on the scales after returning to Texas. To our considerable shock we both found that we had *lost* several pounds instead of gaining weight.

In spite of the fact that we had not denied ourselves in any way, we could only attribute this pleasant surprise to the fact that we were eating organic foods that were so flavorful that we were subconsciously content to each notably smaller portions than are typically served in Texas.

Learning from our adventures described in the preceding pages however, there are a number of things that my wife and I would choose to do differently on our next trip.

First and foremost we would ensure that we were supplied with the camper van that we selected. And the van that we would select would be of the type with a double bed that lowered from the ceiling, thus providing a substantially larger area of useable floor space. While Gisèle had been very serviceable for our needs, the combination of her "night crawler" bed configuration and narrow passageway became rather tedious after 22 nights in succession. We would also ensure that our next rental van was equipped with the retractable awning that would have not only served to expand our living space but would have also provided shelter from both the rain and sun that we encountered during our journey. And each day's journey would start with a check of the skylights followed by a verbal reminder to one another of the vertical clearance height of the vehicle!

Another area with considerable room for improvement was in the planning of our daily itinerary as we followed *Le Tour*. Although due the very nature of the race we would need to travel substantial distances on certain days as we moved from one stage to the next, I could have done a much better job of planning these relocations. On numerous occasions we found ourselves bound by our schedule and unable to spend the time to take in the experiences offered by our surroundings. Missing out on visiting the Normandy beaches and finding my great-great-uncle's grave are just two examples of the imbalance caused by my inflexible planning. In addition we should have taken advantage of the many online resources available to help us research each region of the country that we were to visit, thereby identifying in advance local culinary specialties and sites of particular interest.

Although there are literally thousands of campgrounds in France, I had convinced myself while planning our journey that it was imperative to reserve each night's accommodation well in advance. I soon found that I could make such reservations by telephone; however the matter of paying a deposit in advance became problematic because most campground operators required the payment to be made by electronic bank draft in Euros. Rather than face making a series of payments in this manner, I decided instead to limit myself to choosing those campgrounds that could be reserved over the internet with payment by credit card. Even though this approach limited the number of available campgrounds, it proved to be much simpler than arranging bank transfers.

But after all of these painstaking efforts from afar, we learned that there really was no need whatsoever to have reserved in advance because there was plenty of room available in campgrounds all over the country. Of the ten campgrounds in which we stayed during our journey, only one had been close to full when we arrived. After our arrival in France we could simply have bought one of the many available campground guidebooks and achieved a much more flexible schedule by choosing our overnight location each day according to our needs at the time.

Another lesson learned was with regard to the toll road system. In all we spent around US $400 on *autoroute* tolls during our 5,000 kilometer journey around France. Probably around half of those kilometers were tallied on one *autoroute* or another which means that we paid around 16 cents per kilometer (or 26 cents per mile) for the privilege of using the admittedly smooth and well-maintained freeways of France. But not only did our money buy us a smooth journey, it also provided a great deal of entertainment for us as we watched our credit card be declined followed in turn by the joyful experience of fiddling around with coins while the drivers of vehicles behind us grew ever more impatient. Although there is nothing that can be done about the price of the tolls, an electronic toll tag would make our next driving sojourn in France much less complicated.

On a similar note, a microchip-enabled credit card would also have saved us a number of delays and moments of embarrassment during our stay in France. Both a card of this type and an electronic toll tag could have been obtained in advance if I had done my homework properly during the 9 months or so that I was planning the trip.

But I am happy to report that we were able to solve one particular problem during our three weeks in France, that of gaining portable wireless access to the internet. Visiting the nearest McDonalds restaurant simply for the purpose of using their free Wi-Fi service felt dishonest, and buying fast food there felt like we were betraying the spirit of our intentions to enjoy all things French. Eventually it was my wife who found the perfect solution. About a week before we were due to return to Paris, she suggested I pay a visit to a cell phone store that she had noticed next to the supermarket she was about to enter.

No sooner than I had explained my particular need to the store manager, she disappeared into a back room and returned with a small white plastic box about the size of a deck of cards. *Voilà! Le Web Trotter!* This inexpensive little unit allowed us to connect to the internet from any location within range of a cell phone tower. As a side benefit I think it also contributed to our overall weight loss during the trip because it allowed us to stay away from McDonalds.

However there is one aspect of our recent trip to France that I will assuredly not change on any future visit to *Le Tour*. I will absolutely, positively *not* bring my bike with me. I have seen those mountain roads up close along with the highly-trained athletes who navigate them for hours on end powered only by their own muscle power and determination. I'm here to tell you – that bike race really *is* harder than it looks!

ABOUT THE AUTHOR

Steve Banner spent most of his working career in adult education in the telecommunications industry before changing his path to tax and accounting, and then finally to his longed-for field of travel writing. He counts himself blessed to have two wonderful children and to be married to his very supportive and patient wife.

21910794R00115

Made in the USA
San Bernardino, CA
11 June 2015